SHADOWS IN THE MIST

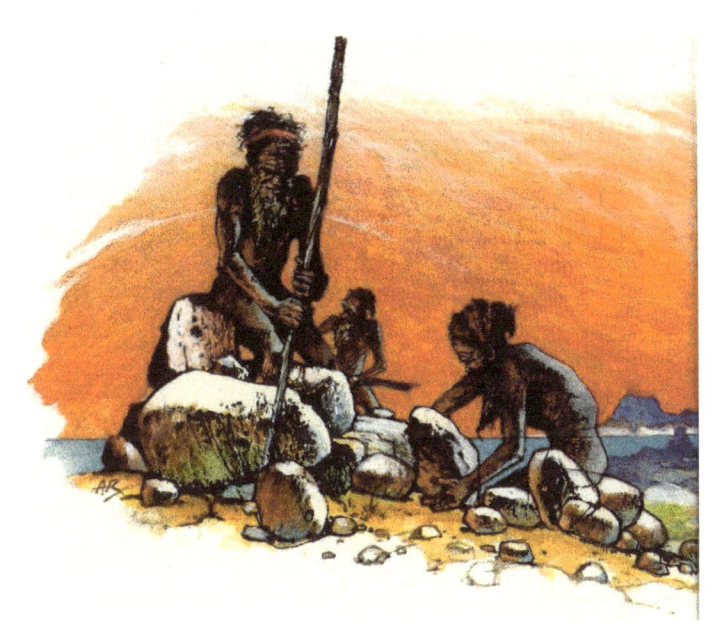

TO THE AUSTRALIAN ABORIGINES
who handed down these Dreamtime Myths

SHADOWS IN THE MIST

AUSTRALIAN ABORIGINAL MYTHS IN PAINTINGS

BY AINSLIE ROBERTS
AND TEXT BY DALE ROBERTS

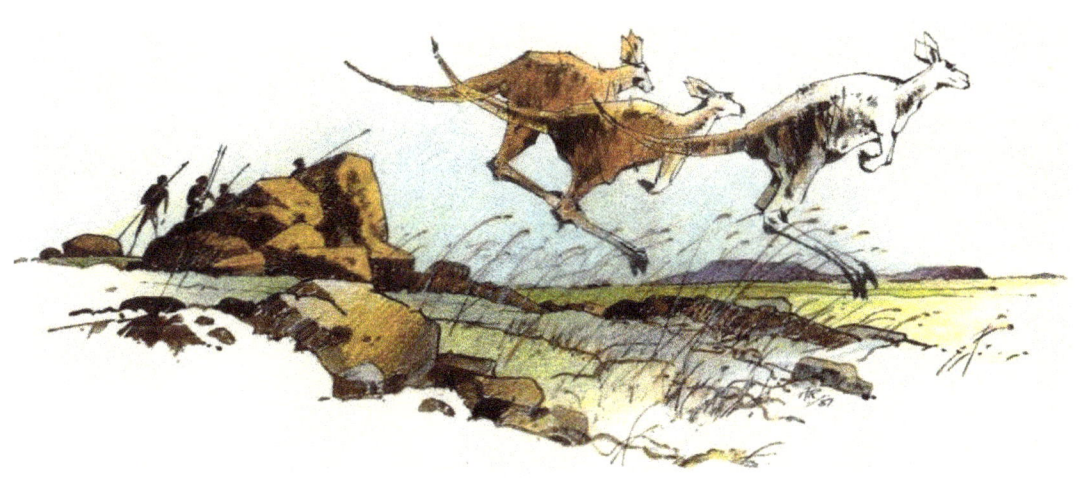

ETT IMPRINT

Exile Bay

First published by ETT Imprint, Exile Bay in 2021

Paintings and drawings by Ainslie Roberts
Text by Dale Roberts
First published by Rigby in 1989. Reprinted 1990.
First electronic edition ETT Imprint 2021

Copyright © Rhys Roberts 2021

This book is copyright. Apart from any fair dealing for the purposes of private study, research, criticism or review, as permitted under the Copyright Act, no part may be reproduced by any process without written permission. Enquiries should be addressed to the publisher, or by email on ettimprint@hotmail.com

ETT IMPRINT
PO Box R1906
Royal Exchange NSW 1225
Australia

ISBN 978-1-922473-91-2 (pback)

ISBN 978-1-922473-92-9 (ebook)

Designed by Rhys Roberts

Cover: The Rain Dragon, by Ainslie Roberts

Contents

Introduction 6
The First Birth 8
The Stolen Grinding Stones 10
Unwara's Web of Death 12
Bubbles of Life 14
The Origin of Spencer Gulf 16
Jitta-jitta and Kubiri 18
The Blessing of Fire 20
Kookaburra and the Rainbow Serpent 22
Creation of the Milky Way 24
Birth of the Seals 26
The Kosciusko Bogong Moth 28
The Desert Ice-men 30
Trees Born of Fire 32
The Burning Cormorant 34
Birth of the Opal 36
The Guardian of Owl Rock 38
Birthplace of the Moons 40
The Search for Moodai 42
Wira Reborn 44
Wungala and the Evil-Big-Eyed-One.... 46
Eerin the Protector 48
Storm Warning 50
Kalala the Fire-Tailed Finch 52
The Rain Dragon 54
The Rainmakers 56
Darambal of the Dreamtime 58
Banishment of the Goanna 60
Yulu's Charcoal 62
The Eagle and the Dingo 64
The Bonefish Tree 66
Abduction of the White Swans 68
Jirakupai and Herons 70
The First Death 72
Mopaditi 74
The Gymea 76
Man of Magic 78
The Last Hurricane 80
Acknowledgments 82

SHADOWS IN THE MIST

"Coming events cast their shadows before."

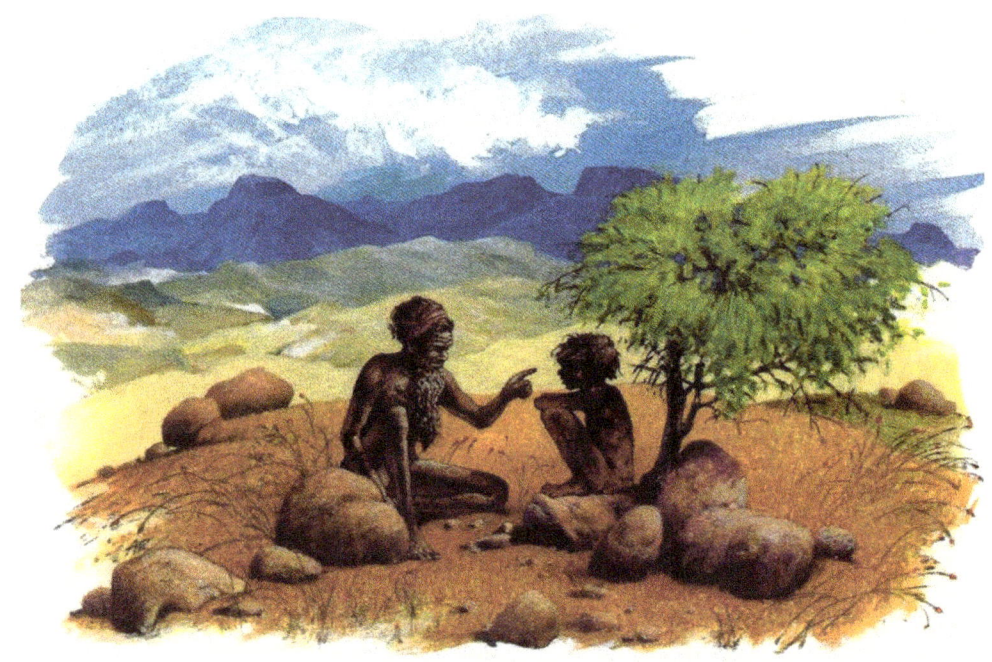

The Macquarie Dictionary defines a shadow as a 'dark figure ... cast on the ground', a 'spectre or ghost', even 'an inseparable companion, one who follows a person in order to keep watch upon him.'

The Dreamtime myths of the Australian Aborigines are indeed an inseparable part of their life and their landscape. Their beliefs, expressed through those myths, form the very basis of their culture.

This book presents a selection of Ainslie Roberts' artistic interpretations of those beliefs.

The mystical conditions known to the Aborigines collectively as the Dreamtime belong to a time in their past – some 40,000 years ago – when their ancestral creators made their world. These creators shaped every feature of the earth: all the hills, the rivers and seas, all the plants and creatures and all the natural forces.

Before this time of creation, Aboriginal earth had always existed as a large flat disc floating in space. Its uninhabited surface was a vast featureless plain, extending unbroken to the horizon. But beneath that monotonous surface were strange indeterminate forms of life that would eventually transform the forbidding landscape.

And so they did. Mythical beings, many resembling giant creatures, began to emerge from out of the mists of time. They wandered all over the earth, shaping it into the world that the Aborigines know today.

But then, suddenly, this Dreamtime came to an end. The great creators had finished their work and disappeared into the shadows of the natural features they had formed.

Today, tribal Aborigines look upon themselves as direct descendants of those mythical beings of the past. Every Aborigine who lives in the country created by his Dreamtime ancestors is linked intimately with that environment. It is a very close personal link that dominates his entire philosophy, code of behaviour and way of life. It is the foundation of all his social, secular and ceremonial activities. As it was done in the Dreamtime, so it must be done today.

Ainslie Roberts' paintings dramatically demonstrate this intense affinity of the Aborigines with their land. For nearly forty years he has been deeply involved with Aboriginal culture, a culture he long ago recognised as rich and vital, deserving to be noticed, respected and explored. Indeed, his paintings reproduced in this book vividly bring to life the myths of that culture.

These are not Aboriginal paintings. They are a white man's interpretation of the ancient stories which provide the Aborigines with a logical explanation of the world in which they live. Their myths define the origin of every topographical feature and the creation of life in all its forms. Wind, rain, sun, fire, rocks, water, birds and beasts - all have a specific reason for being.

But the most important of the Aboriginal creation stories are those which decree the rules of behaviour that all must obey to ensure the harmonious functioning of their society. These laws are clearly outlined in the Dreamtime mythology.

This mythology is eternal. It identifies Aboriginal past, present and future. For the great Dreamtime ancestors are an integral part of the land and life. They exist in all things and speak to those who know how to listen, leaving signposts for those who have learned how to read them, following, guiding, always there as the shadows in the mist.

THE FIRST BIRTH

The mystery of the origins of the Universe has fascinated man since time began. All races - peoples of all colours and cultures - have legends to describe the creation of the world. Scientists would have us believe in a theory of evolution. Others have looked to their gods or some greater being for explanations.

The Australian Aborigines believe that in the beginning, the earth was flat and featureless, unbroken by any mountain range, river or major natural feature. This barren waste was totally uninhabited. There was no light, no living creature, not even a blade of grass to disturb that dim, mute immensity. There was no sound of wind. Nothing moved.

Then, at some time in the long-distant past which the Aborigines call the Dreamtime, giant beings began to wander over the country. As they travelled, these Dreamtime heroes carried out the same tasks that the Aborigines do today. They camped, made fire, dug for water, fought each other and performed ceremonies.

The Tiwi tribe of Melville Island tell the creation myth of Mudungkala. It relates how suddenly, out of the darkness, came a great upheaval of rock and earth. The vast featureless face of the land moved and cracked as the landscape erupted with life and sound. And from the depths emerged an old blind woman, Mudungkala, clutching her three children, a son, Purukupali, and two daughters, Wuriupranala and Murupiangkala, to her breast.

Carrying her children, she crawled along the land, in the process forming all the watercourses. When she had finished, she disappeared. But before she left, she decreed that the bare land she had created should be clothed with vegetation and populated with creatures so that her children, whom she was leaving behind, and the generations to come, should have ample food and shelter.

And so her two daughters and son established themselves in the new land. The journey of life had begun.

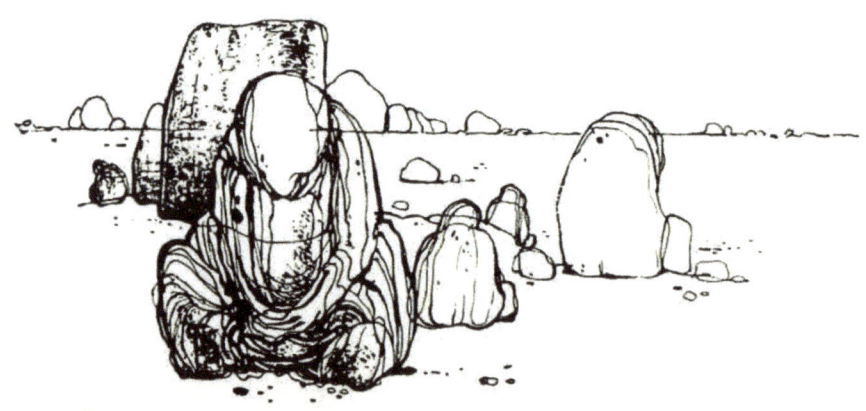

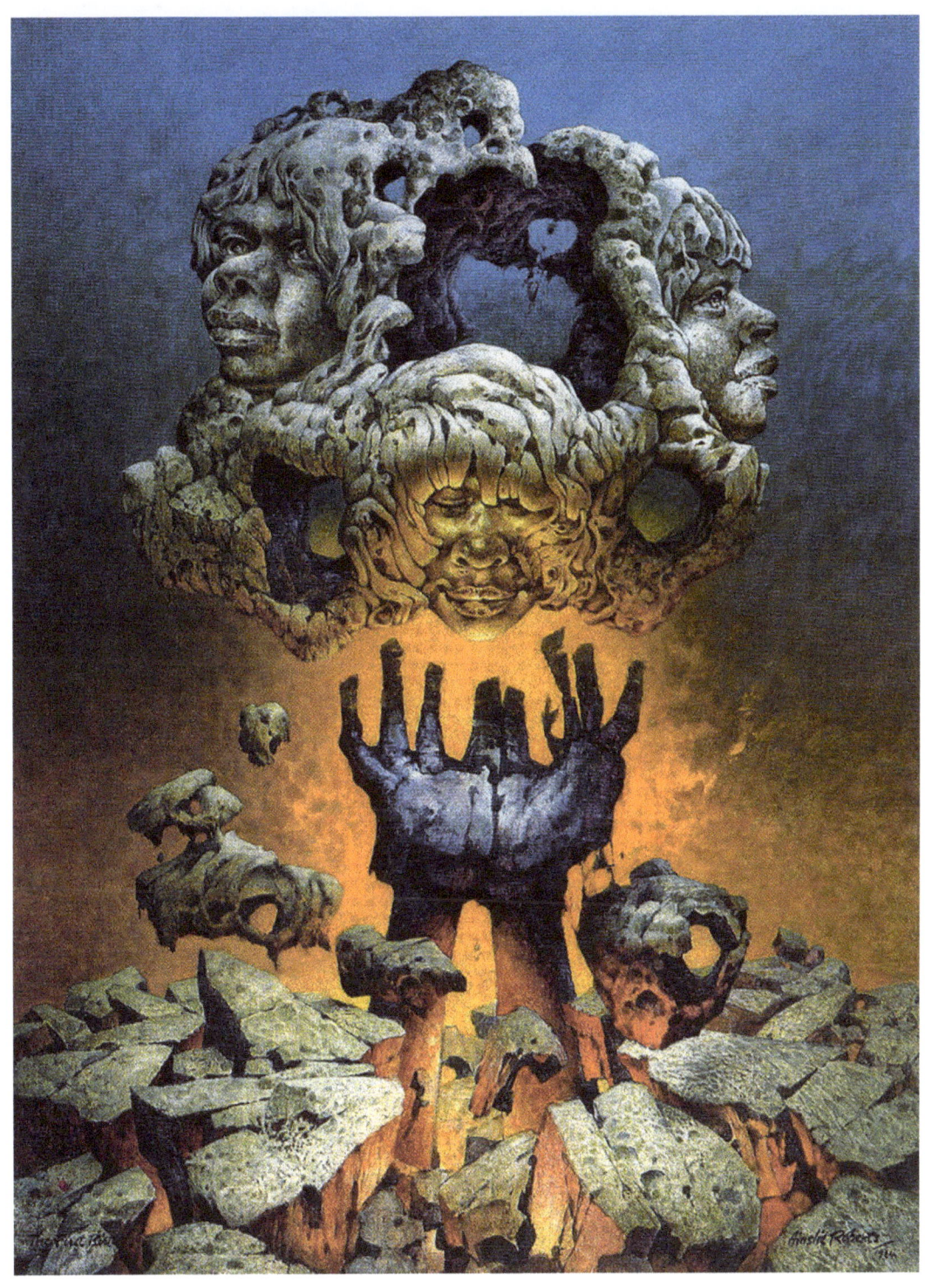

Mr Samuel and Mys Wendy Olenik

THE STOLEN GRINDING STONES

In the cities of Australia today, the hi-tech home is packed with the latest labour-saving devices, wonderful gadgets and gizmos that chop, slice, peel and cook food faster than ever before.

But hi-tech plays little part in the lives of the Australian Aborigines. These people have always been a hunting and food-gathering race. Their tools and weapons, made only from wood and stone, are the simplest owned by any living community.

The women of the tribe regularly grind seeds into flour. Aborigines of South Australia have travelled for centuries to Prism Hill in the Flinders Ranges for the large slabs of sandstone found there with which to make the bottom grinding stones.

For long ago in the Dreamtime, a little woman, Kurakuka, of the dove totem, lived near Tirika Tiru Kura, the place known today as Frome Well in the Flinders Ranges. She had a pair of grinding stones of which she was very proud and every day she would collect and grind seeds.

But there was a pigeon-man, Mutamuta, in that country who used to watch Kurakuka with envy and often longed to have her stones. One day, when Kurakuka was out hunting with the rest of the women of her tribe, Mutamuta stole the large bottom grinding stone and, changing into the bronze-winged pigeon, flew away with it. But the weight of the stone was too much for him and he dropped it at Vinbituna, a place close to Prism Hill.

Kurakuka cried so much over the loss of her large grinding stone that she transformed herself into a dove and her eyes are red even to this day. And the pigeon, whenever he begins his flight, makes a sharp clattering noise. This is the sound of the grinding stone that he stole so long ago dragging along the ground as he started to fly off with it back in the Dreamtime.

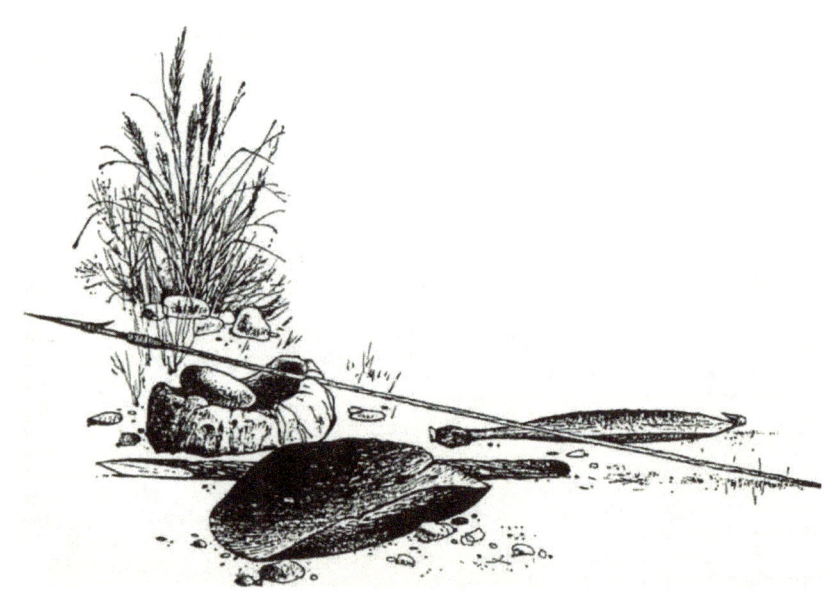

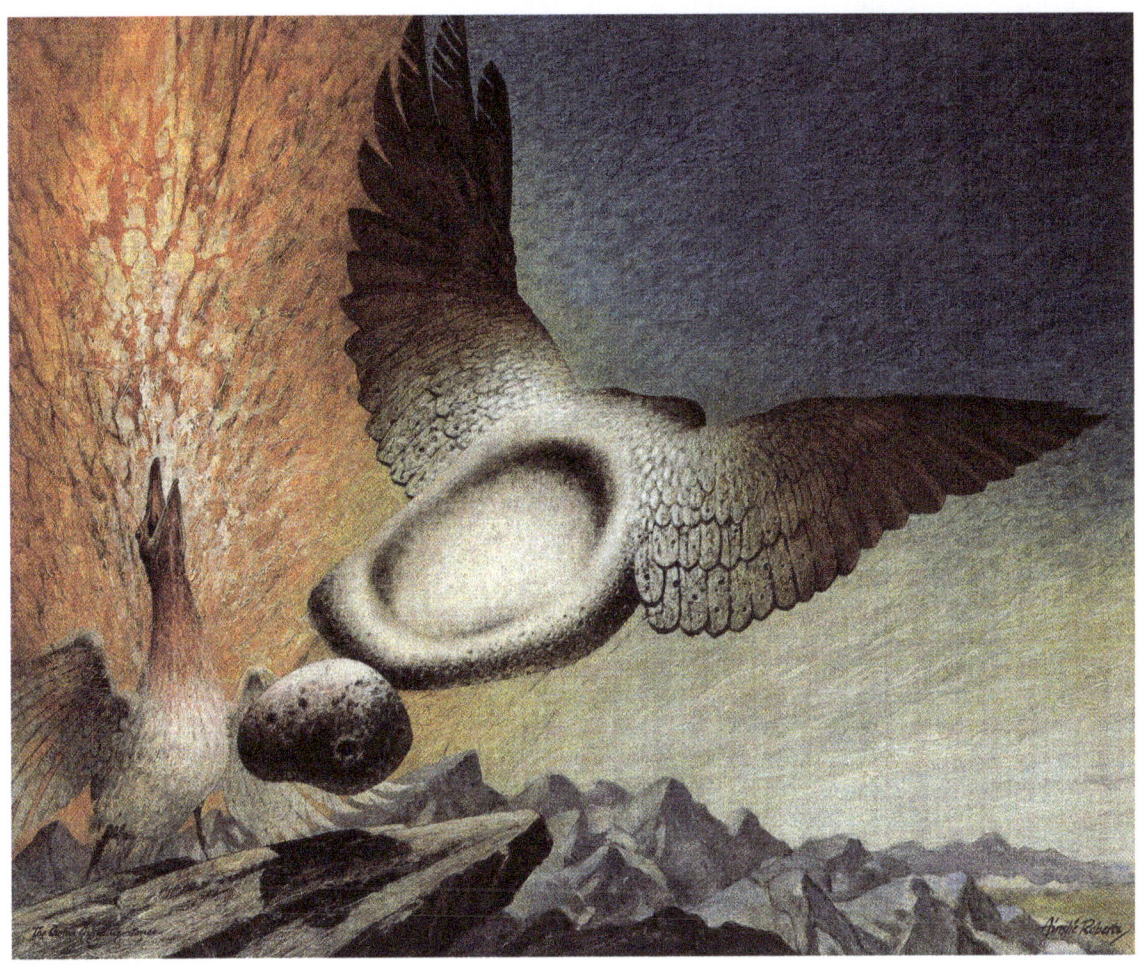

Private Collection

UNWARA'S WEB OF DEATH

Since white man stepped on to Australian soil, he has attempted to impose, without exception, his own brand of law on all the inhabitants of the country.

This has often caused conflict for the Aborigines, for they live within the bounds of tribal laws, laws which are absolute. They may not be broken and the penalties for doing so are harsh.

Many of their myths, such as this one told by the tribes of the Lake Eyre region, stand as reminders of the rules.

Unwara, an old Spider-man, was guardian of his two nephews, Nali and Balinga. He was also a very clever medicine-man.

Although they were not yet fully initiated men, Nali and Balinga fell in love with two sisters from a neighbouring tribe and persuaded the girls to come and live in their camp. In doing this, the youths were breaking tribal law. Unwara and the elders were very angry but said nothing about it that night.

The following day, Unwara sent his nephews off in one direction for the day's hunting and the two sisters in another direction to collect grass seeds and yams. As soon as the youths were out of sight, Unwara changed the girls into emus and sent them to feed by a nearby waterhole.

When his nephews returned, Unwara met them calling out excitedly, "Sneak down to the waterhole. There are two emus drinking down there!"

Nali and Balinga quickly stalked and killed the emus because the transformed sisters, recognising the youths, made no attempt to run away. When the nephews brought the dead emus back to camp, Unwara laughed scornfully, telling them they had killed the very girls they had wanted so much.

And because the nephews had disobeyed the tribal law, Unwara and the other elders of the tribe banished Nali and Balinga from the land of their birth forever.

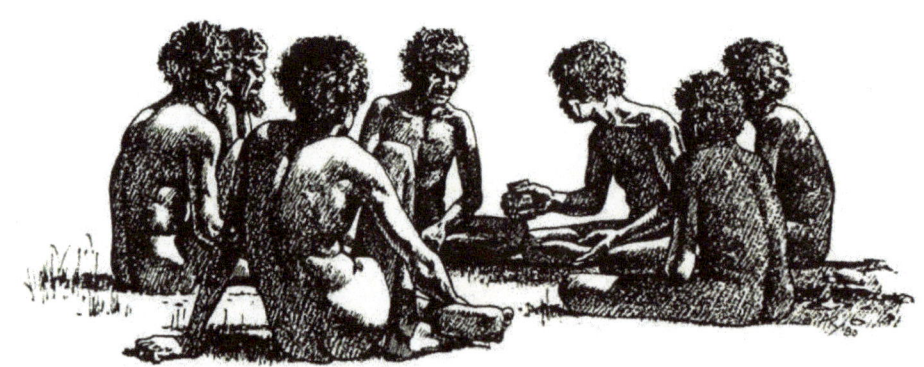

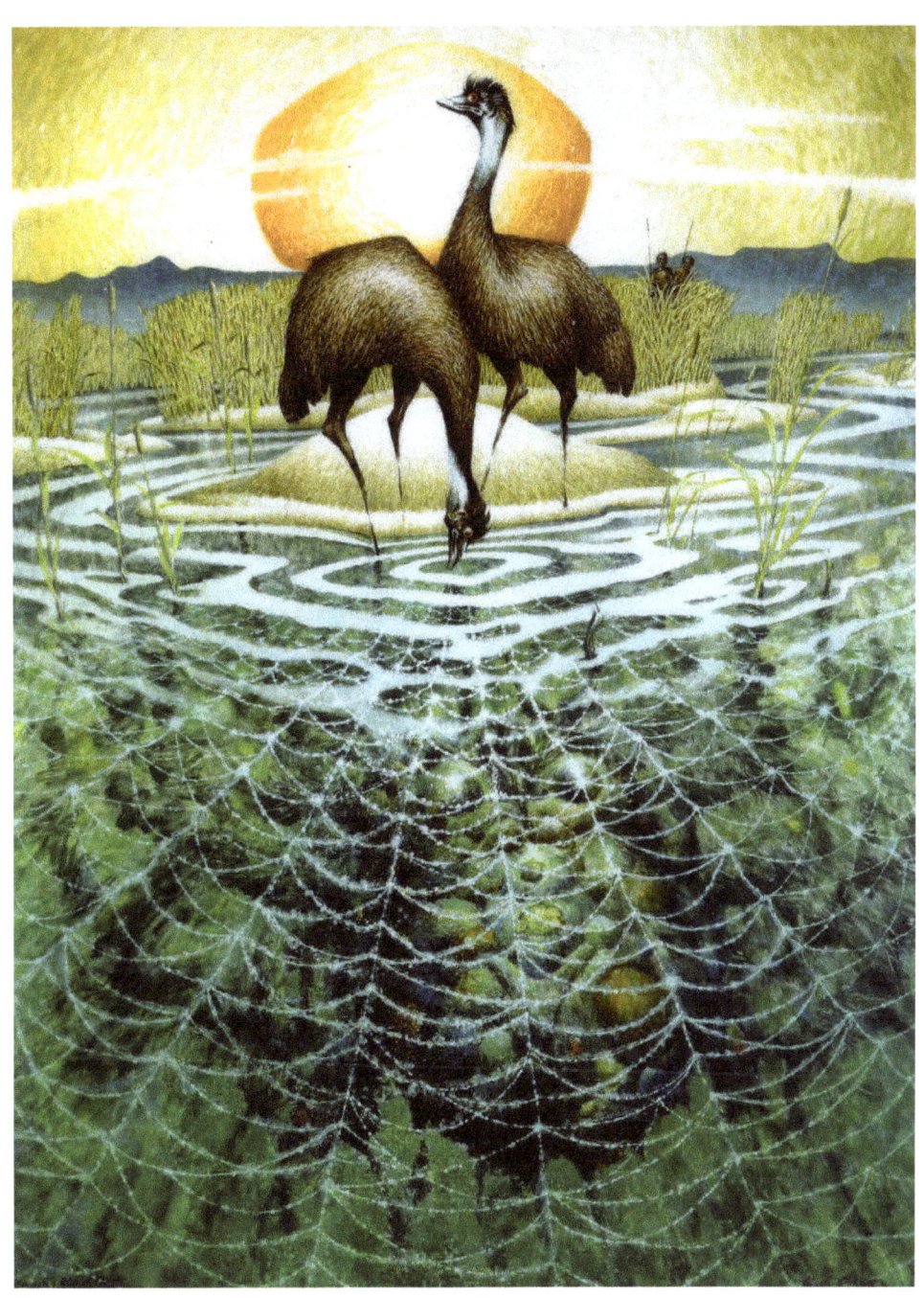

Mr Samuel and Mys Wendy Olenik

BUBBLES OF LIFE

'Truth is stranger than fiction' states the old adage. But in our modern world of perpetual miracles of science, sophisticated man has become almost blasé about the wonders of nature.

One such unexplained marvel is a large fresh water spring bubbling continually in the Arafura Sea, just north of eastern Australia. Its source is unknown; its purity is always unsalted.

But to the Aborigines it is no freak, no mystery. For they believe that in creation times a man, Duandja, and his family lived on the sea coast near the mouth of the Liverpool River in Arnhem land.

One day, Duandja made a bark canoe and, putting his family aboard, set out to visit a distant island. But when they were far out to sea, a heavy storm of rain and wind swamped the canoe and it sank.

When they reached the bottom of the sea, Duandja decided that it was an excellent place. The family set up camp and Duandja lit a camp fire. But the Fire gave off no smoke. Instead, rising from the flames was a stream of water bubbles. When Duandja tasted them he found they were fresh, so he sent them to the surface so that his friends could, on a long canoe journey, get a drink if they became thirsty.

Ever since that time, a spring of fresh water bubbles up in the sea right over the centre of Duandja's camp. Should the Aborigines run short of water when they are on a canoe journey anywhere off the coast from the Liverpool River, they paddle to the spring of fresh water, fill their water vessels and quench their thirst.

To this day, Duandja and his family keep careful watch over the camp fire for, should it go out, the stream of fresh water bubbles would cease forever. This fresh water spring in the Arafura Sea covers a considerable area and appears to be constant.

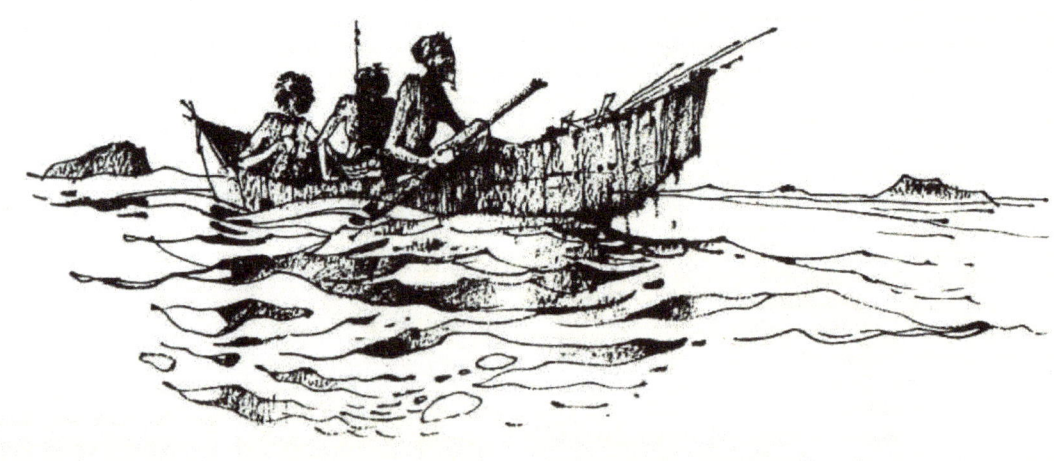

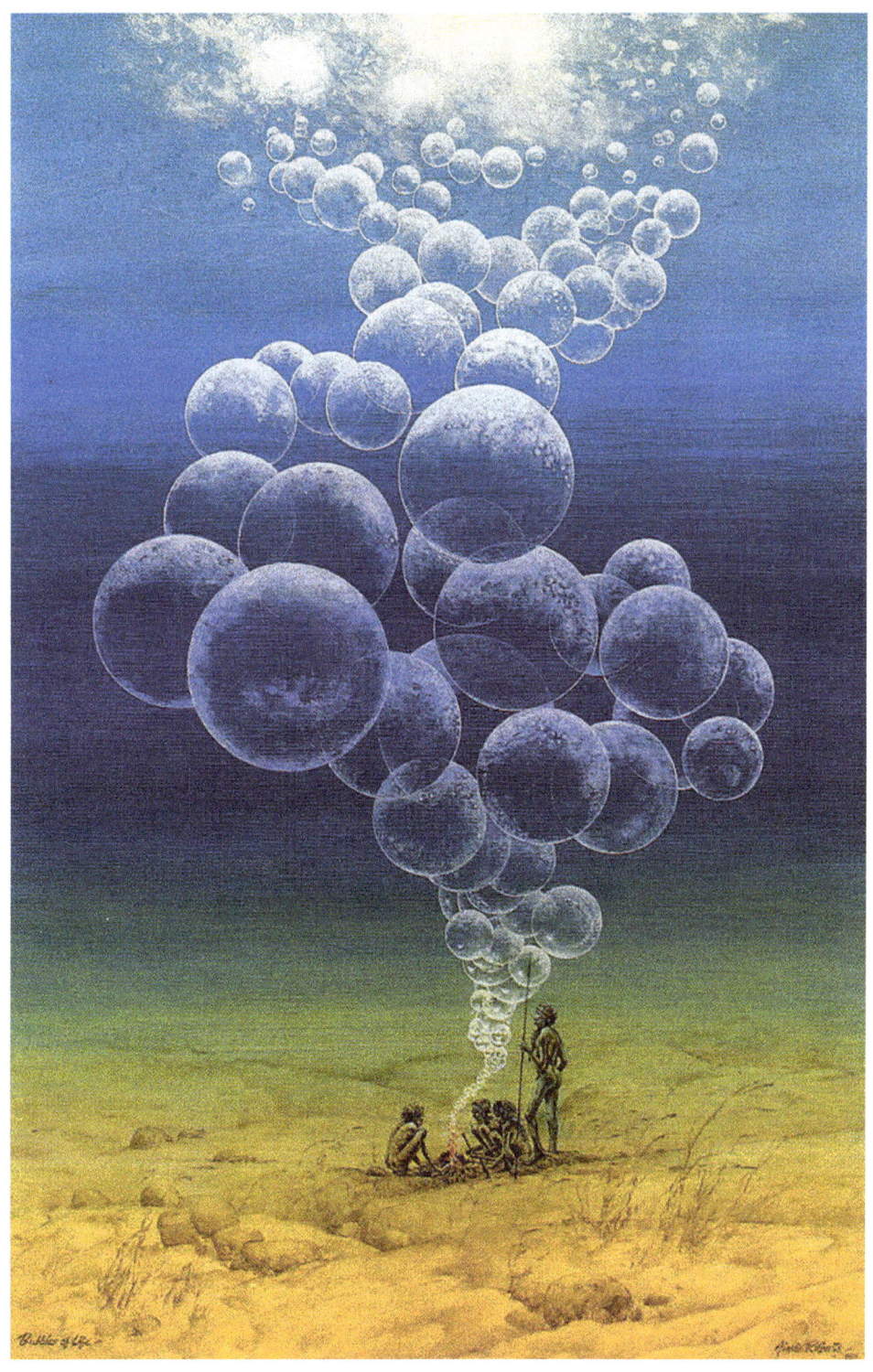

Private Collection

THE ORIGIN OF SPENCER GULF

Modern education has tried to keep pace with our rapidly developing world. Not so long ago, geography was the skill of memorising the names of the capital cities and rivers of countries of the world. Today it is all 'topography' and 'continental drift', scientific explanations for features fashioned by nature.

Geography for the Australian Aborigines is a matter of believing that all the natural features of their land have a reason for being. They were all created in the Dreamtime for a specific purpose.

Spencer Gulf, in South Australia, was once a valley filled with a line of fresh water lagoons stretching northwards for more than two hundred kilometres. Each lagoon was the exclusive territory of a species of water bird. The trees belonged to the eagles, crows and parrots, while in the open country between the lagoons lived emus, curlews and mallee fowls. In the thick grass by the waters were snakes, goannas and lizards while the animals lived further out.

For a long time all lived in harmony. But trouble started when the birds, because of their greater numbers, more beautiful appearance and their ability to fly, felt so superior that they prohibited the animals and reptiles from drinking at the lagoons. Thus began a long conflict in which many were killed or died of thirst.

In those days, the kangaroo was a man who grieved over the unnecessary fighting. Finally he decided that if an opening could be made in the southern isthmus which in those days blocked the sea from entering the valley, the conflict would be ended by the flooding of the lagoons.

Now the kangaroo-man possessed the thigh bone of a mythical ancestor. With this bone he had already performed many wonderful deeds. So he pointed the bone at the isthmus which slowly split open. The sea poured through the opening, flooding the entire valley so that the birds and the animals were forced to live together in peace.

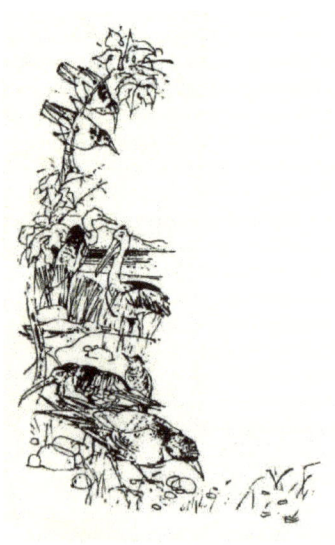

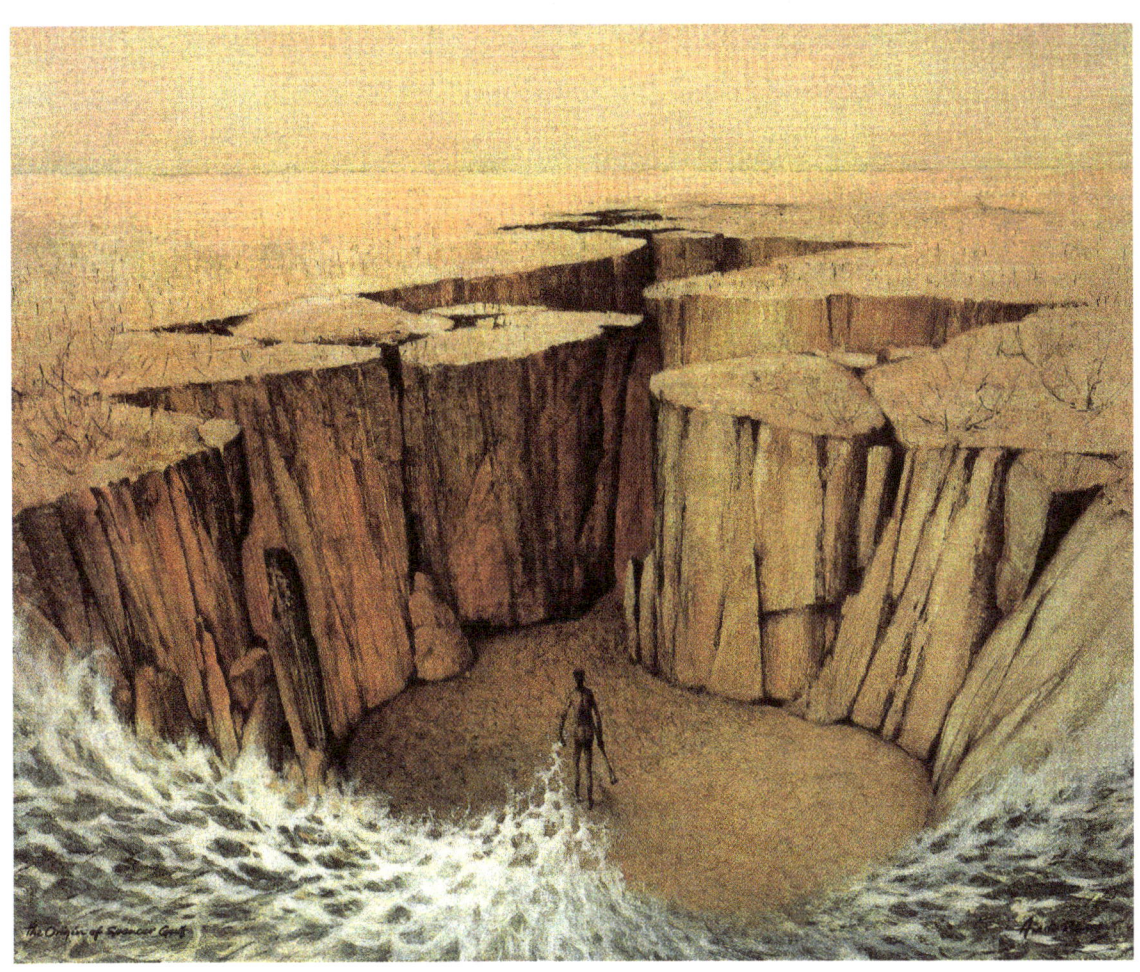

The State Bank of South Australia

JITTA-JITTA AND KUBIRI

Many other Dreamtime ancestral heroes appear in Aboriginal mythology as birds, birds which are still today honoured by some tribes.

This ancient story comes from a mountainous area of Western Australia where there are many caves. One of these caves was the home of a giant man-eating dingo and another that of a huge snake. Every morning these creatures emerged to roam the country and raid the Aborigines' camps in search of victims.

The only large waterhole in the area was close to the caves. The tribes lost so many of their people who tried to collect water there that they had to depend on what little water they could collect after rains. They dared not light fires to cook their meat or to warm themselves lest the snake and dingo follow the scent of cooking to its source. As a result of these hardships, more and more of the people were becoming weak, ill and dejected.

But a willy-wagtail-man, Jitta-jitta, and a robin-man, Kubiri, both resourceful hunters, decided to put an end to the suffering. They discussed many desperate plans. At last, one evening when the hot winds were blowing strongly from the north, Kubiri said to Jitta-jitta, "Tomorrow at dawn, we will light a big fire outside the dingo's cave. This wind will fill the cave with smoke. It might blind the dingo long enough for us to kill it when it runs out."

So Jitta-jitta followed their plan and it worked. One lucky blow from his club killed the blundering dingo instantly. But Jitta-jitta had to do it all alone. Kubiri had made a brave speech the previous evening, but when the time came for action, he climbed a nearby tree, shivering with fright and feeling thoroughly ashamed of himself. However, during that day, poor Kubiri's courage j returned. He set out alone on the following morning and used the same trick to destroy the great snake. When the Dreamtime ended and the two men were transformed into birds, tribal law decreed that neither Jitta-jitta the willy-wagtail nor Kubiri the robin shall ever be killed or molested in any way.

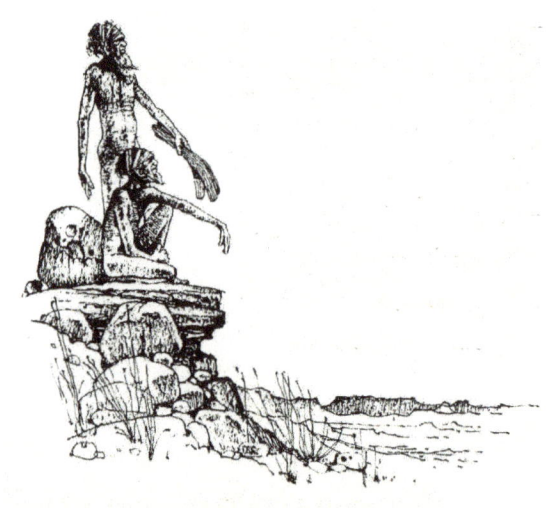

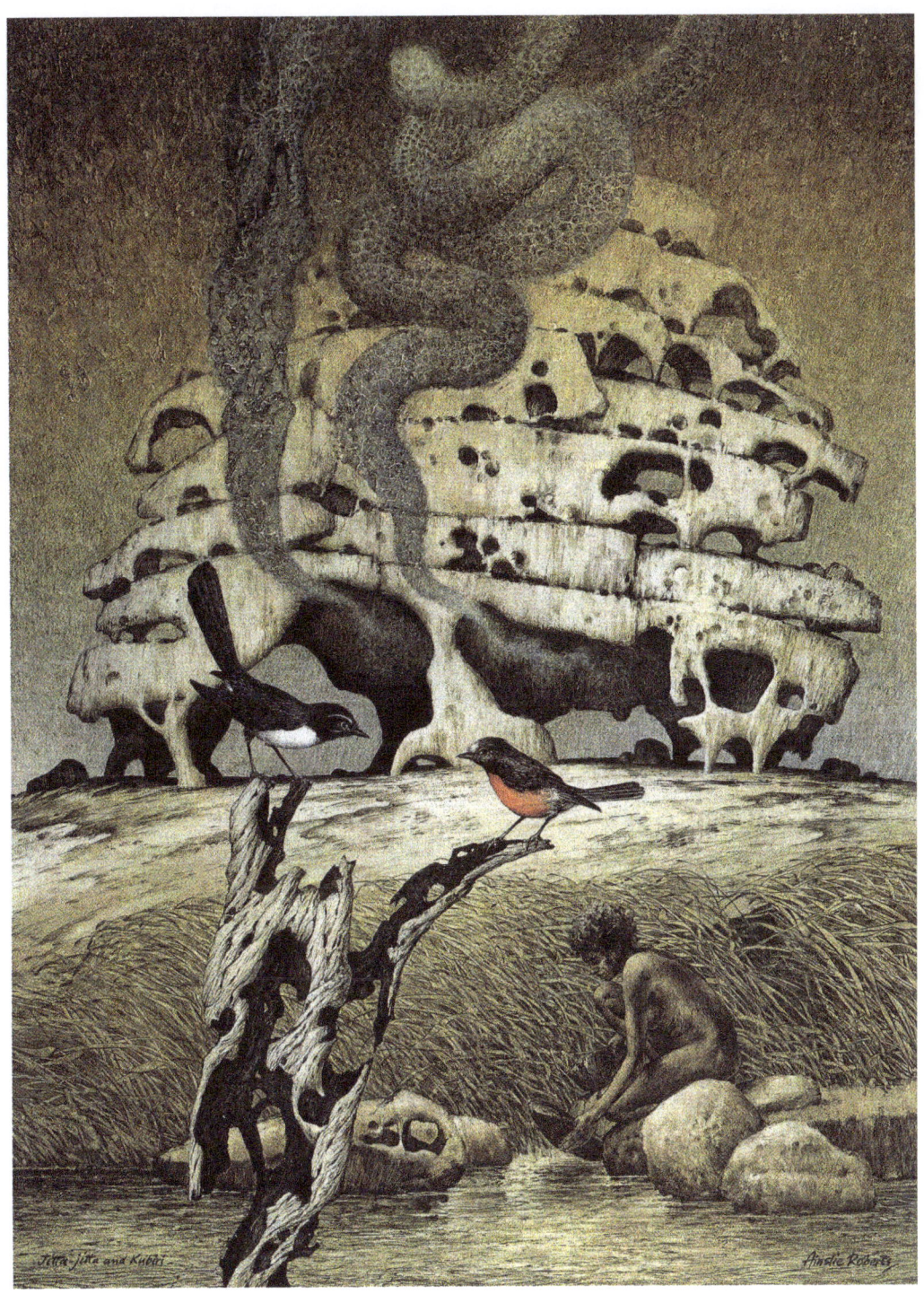

Mr and Mrs D R Wilson

THE BLESSING OF FIRE

Remember the last power blackout? How inconvenient it was. No light, no heat, no TV, not even the microwave to cook the evening meal.

Modern man is indeed frighteningly dependent on the generation of power to fuel both his domestic and industrial needs. For most city dwellers, long gone are the days of squinting in the candle light or huddling by a meagre wood fire.

The Australian Aborigines believe that in the beginning there was no fire and the only light in the world was that from the stars. One of their many variations of the origin of fire is this myth from the time when the earth was cold and clothed in darkness.

But one day, after a heavy thunderstorm, a man and his wife saw a strange glow where a bolt of lightning had struck an old log. Puzzled by this weird sight, they covered it with bark in an attempt to hide it, but the bark suddenly burst into flame. This frightened them so much that they went to their tribal leader, a noted man of magic, and asked him to destroy the strange thing they had found.

But when they returned to the now blazing log and felt the comfort of its warmth, the elder realised that here was something that would give his people light to dispel their darkness and heat to keep them warm.

He gave a large torch of blazing wood to the woman and a smaller torch to the man. And so that the twin blessings of light and warmth would never be lost, he sent them up into the sky to become the sun and the moon. He divided the rest of the burning log amongst the tribe and told them to place a coal in every tree so that the spirit of fire would always be available to everyone.

With fire to cook their food, keep them warm and light their darkness, life became so much easier that the Aborigines increased in numbers and gradually spread over their new land. The use of fire not only altered man's way of life, but set him apart from the rest of creation.

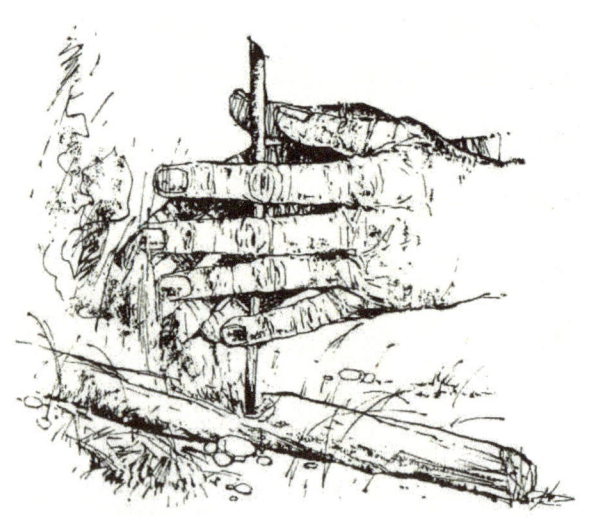

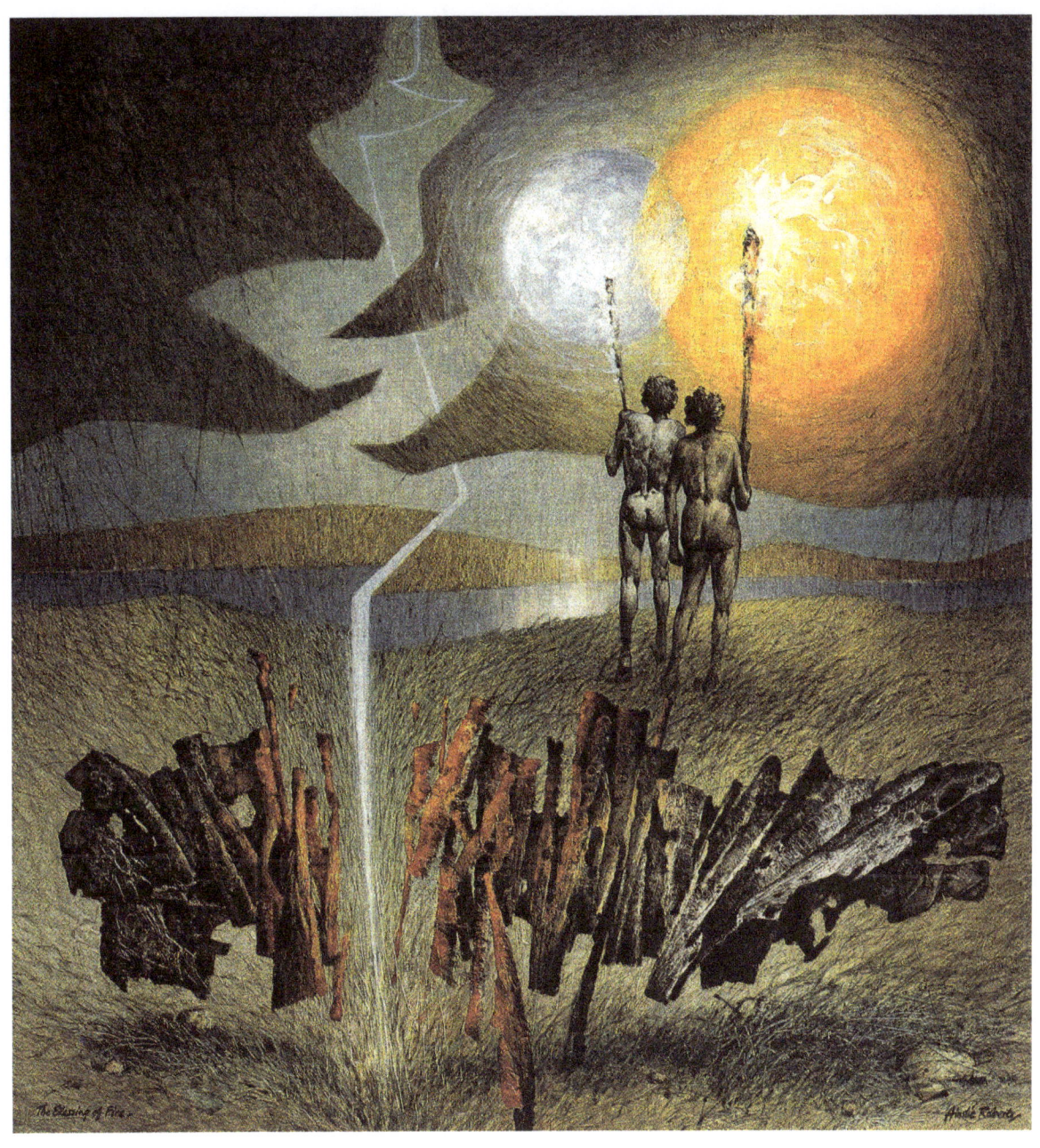

Mrs Melva Roberts

KOOKABURRA AND THE RAINBOW SERPENT

In the mythology of the Australian Aborigines, the most widespread of their beliefs was in the existence of a huge serpent which lived in waterholes, swamps and lakes. In most myths, it was associated with the rainbow. Rainbow serpent myths are Australia-wide, but the greatest variety came from northern Australia where the thunder clouds and violent rains of the monsoonal season provided the ideal environment.

Many myths describe a huge, brilliantly coloured snake that spent the dry season resting in a deep waterhole. In the wet season, it went up into the sky as a rainbow. Usually it was an object of fear to the Aborigines, and great care was taken not to annoy or offend the mighty snake. Should anyone disturb its rest, the rainbow serpent would inevitably create some disaster, from simply eating the offender to making the waterhole overflow and drowning everyone.

In some myths, the rainbow serpent appears as an ancestral creator. Its body contained all the natural features of the land which, in that remote time, was flat and featureless.

This horrific beast sat bloated and replete, all the mountains, rivers, rocks, trees, birds and animals nestled inside it. And until it died, all these beauties of the world were denied to the Aborigines.

Many attempts were made to kill the serpent, but all had failed.

Finally, annoyed that one so greedy should deprive all others, a small and wily Dream time ancestor changed himself into the blue-winged kookaburra. Dazzled by the spectacular sight of this new creature, the fat serpent let it fly so close that the kookaburra was at last able to spear the beast and release all the natural features into the world.

Today, the serpent's spirit appears in the sky as the rainbow. And the world is clothed in the beauties it disgorged.

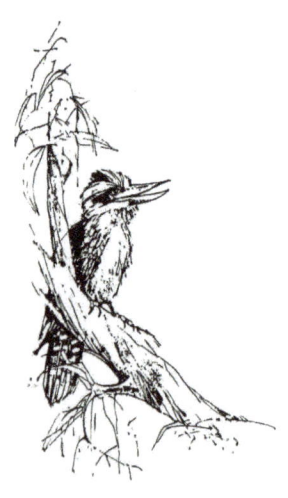

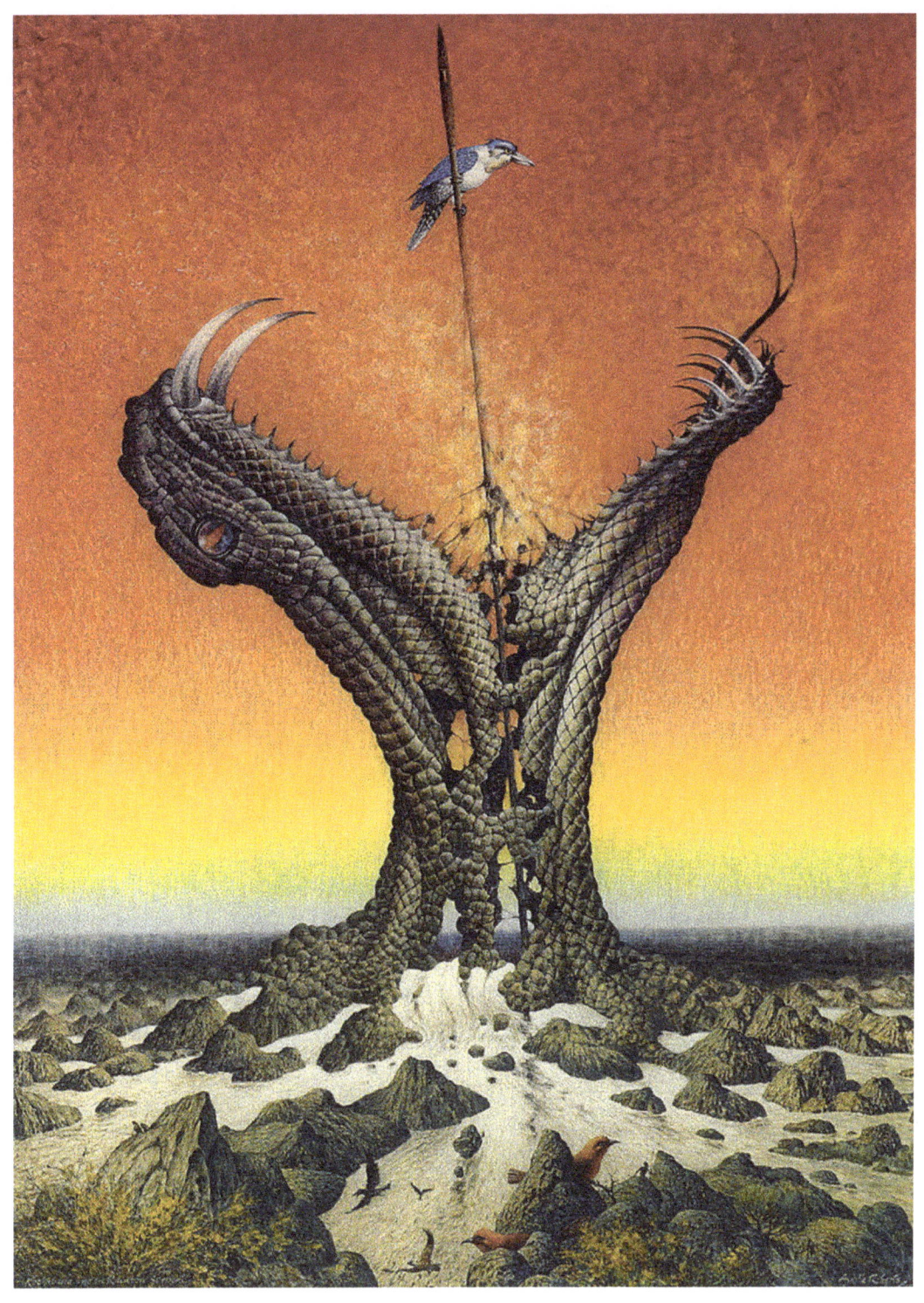

Mr John Lind

CREATION OF THE MILKY WAY

Astronomers assure us that our galaxy, the Milky Way, is a great group of millions of stars shaped like a flat disc with spiral arms. This band of stars stretches across the night sky - myriads of tiny points of light that are really huge balls of hot glowing gas.

The Aborigines who once lived on the shores of Lake Alexandrina at the mouth of the Murray River had a different interpretation. They left behind a number of stories about the exploits of a tall powerful Aboriginal man, Ngurunderi, whom they believe created not only all the fish in the waters of that area but the stars above them.

Ngurunderi was unhappy because his wives had deserted him. He left his camp beside Lake Alexandrina and began to search for them. But when he realized his quest would be over land, he decided he would have no further use for his precious canoe in which he had journeyed so often along the Murray.

Not wishing to abandon so fine a possession and noticing the many parts of the night sky where no stars shone, Ngurunderi resolved to put his canoe to good use.

He selected the two highest sandhills in the area to stand on and lifted his canoe up into one of the dark spots in the sky where it became the bright dusting of stars we call the Milky Way.

Ngurunderi's two sandhills can still be seen at Mount Misery close to the main road. In the language of the jaralde tribe, the word juki means canoe, and so they called the Milky Way Ngurunderi Juki or Ngurunderi's Canoe.

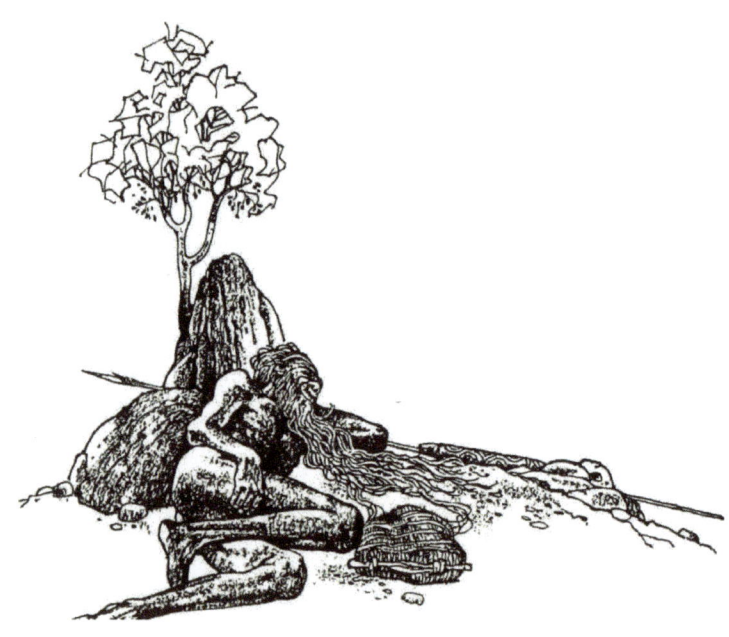

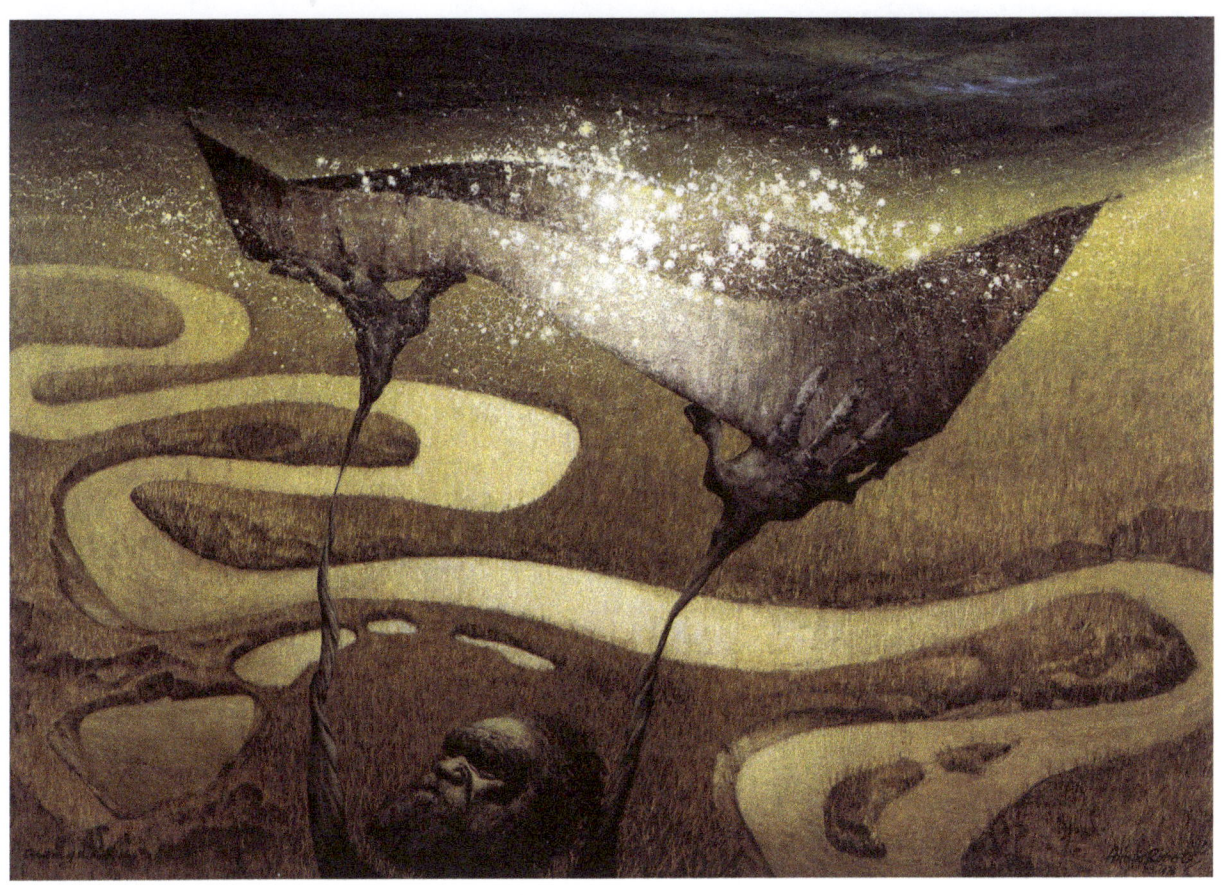

Messrs R, W and C Kemp

BIRTH OF THE SEALS

After placing his canoe into the sky where it became the Milky Way, Ngurunderi set out on foot to recapture his wives. He created many of the natural features of the coastline on his way, the most prominent being a rugged granite headland known today as Rosetta Head or The Bluff.

From this high vantage point, Ngurunderi located his errant wives far to the west. After resting for a while on this headland which the Aborigines later regarded as his sleeping body, Ngurunderi cast four of his spears into the ocean before resuming his chase. Where each spear pierced the water, a rocky island arose.

One of these was Seal Rock, a small island surrounded by dangerous reefs and isolated submerged rocks. And with the creation of Seal Rock came the birth of the hordes of seals which gave the island its name.

For countless centuries, until the coming of the white man, Seal Rock was the birthplace and playground of generations of seals. The white man killed them for their hides, meat and blubber and rapidly reduced their numbers.

Today, there are no seals on Seal Rock. But the haunting cries of the sea birds which nest on it remind us that long ago this was a place where nature was vital and unafraid.

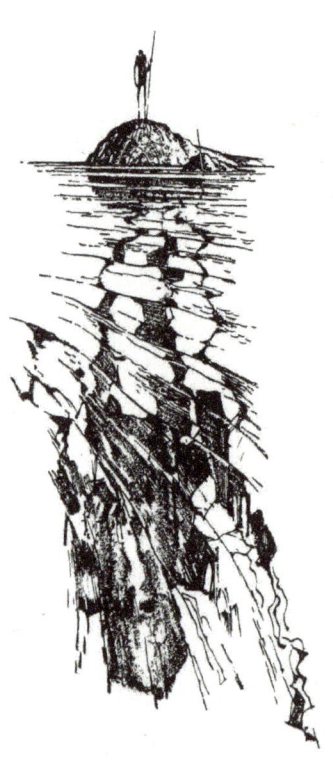

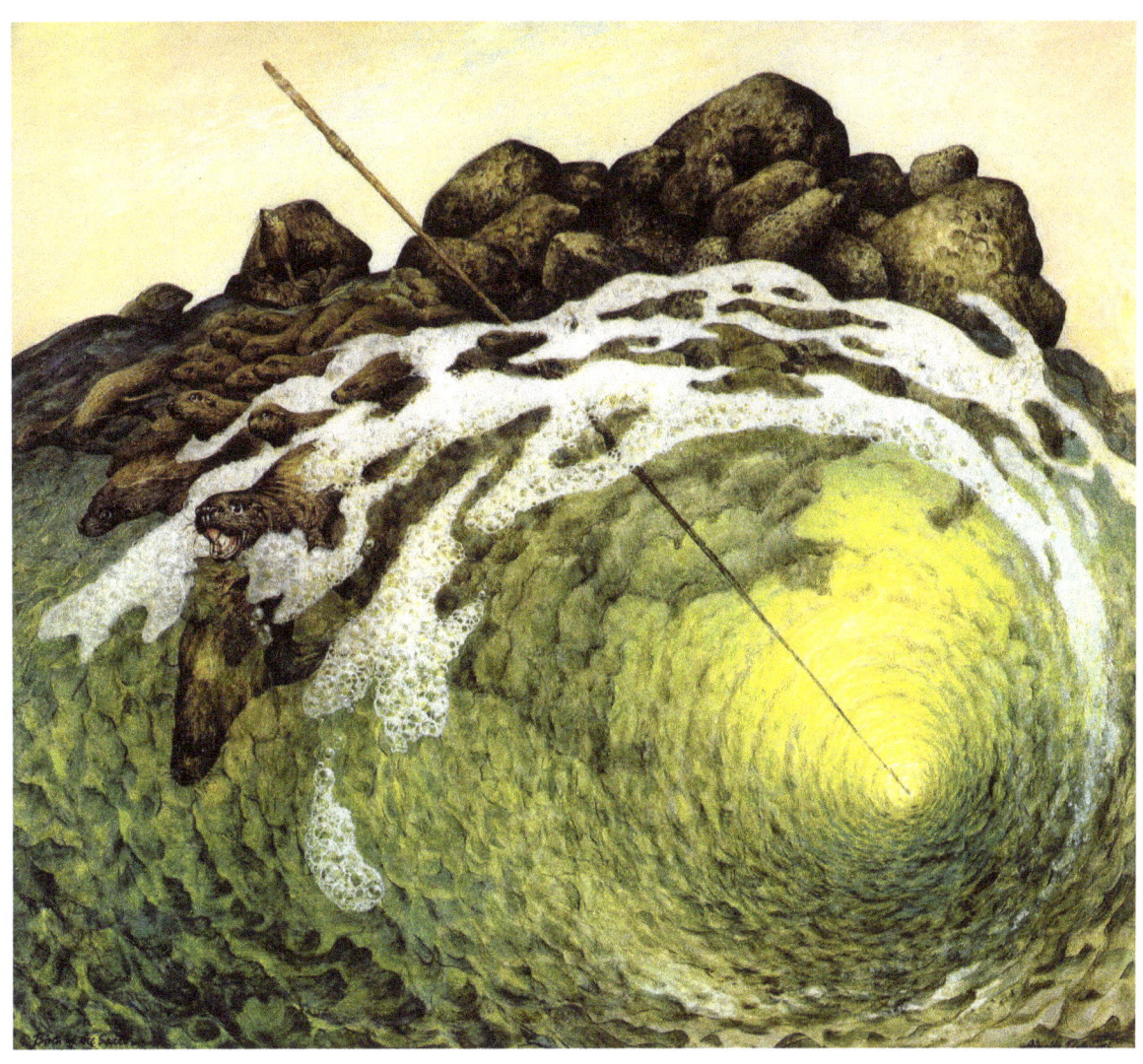

Mr and Mrs Charles E Hulley

THE KOSCIUSKO BOGONG MOTH

Since time immemorial, man has spent some part of each day in the search for food. In primitive tribes, hunger made good hunters. Today the quest is for the cheapest grocery store or the best restaurant. It is all a matter of environment.

The Aborigines of Australia have always known how to live off the land. If it moves, it is food.

For thousands of years, the Bogong moths of the Snowy Mountains were a regular part of the food supply of the Aboriginal tribes in the area through the summer months.

These drab, dull-coloured moths migrate each year to the mountains from the pastures of south-eastern Australia. Collected from their resting places in the granite outcrops, they were roasted in their thousands for their sweet, walnut flavour.

But the Bogong moths were not always dull and drab. Indeed, long ago in the Dreamtime, one of the most beautiful of all creatures was Myee the moth. With her dazzling multi-coloured wings, she lived among the grasses of the river bank. But she often wondered and yearned to find out for herself why the mountains high above her were covered in white.

Her husband, Bogong, often warned her not to leave the safety of the river grasses. But, one day, Myee's curiosity was too much for her and, as the sun was setting, she flew up towards the mountains. As she reached the mountain heights, snow began to fall. The snow beat the fragile Myee to the ground and soon covered her.

Myee did not die. She lay covered by the snow until Spring. But as the snows melted, Myee's beautiful colours also drained away. As they did so, they ran into and coloured the new spring flowers of the mountains.

That is why today the colours of the Bogong moths are generally dull and lifeless, and only the springtime and summer wildflowers of the Mt. Kosciusko region carry the Dreamtime colours of Myee, the first Bogong moth.

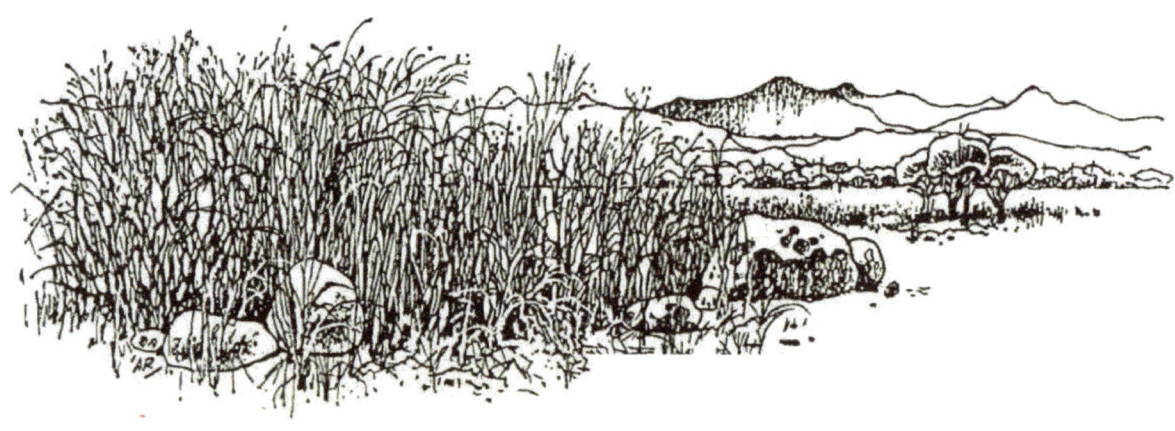

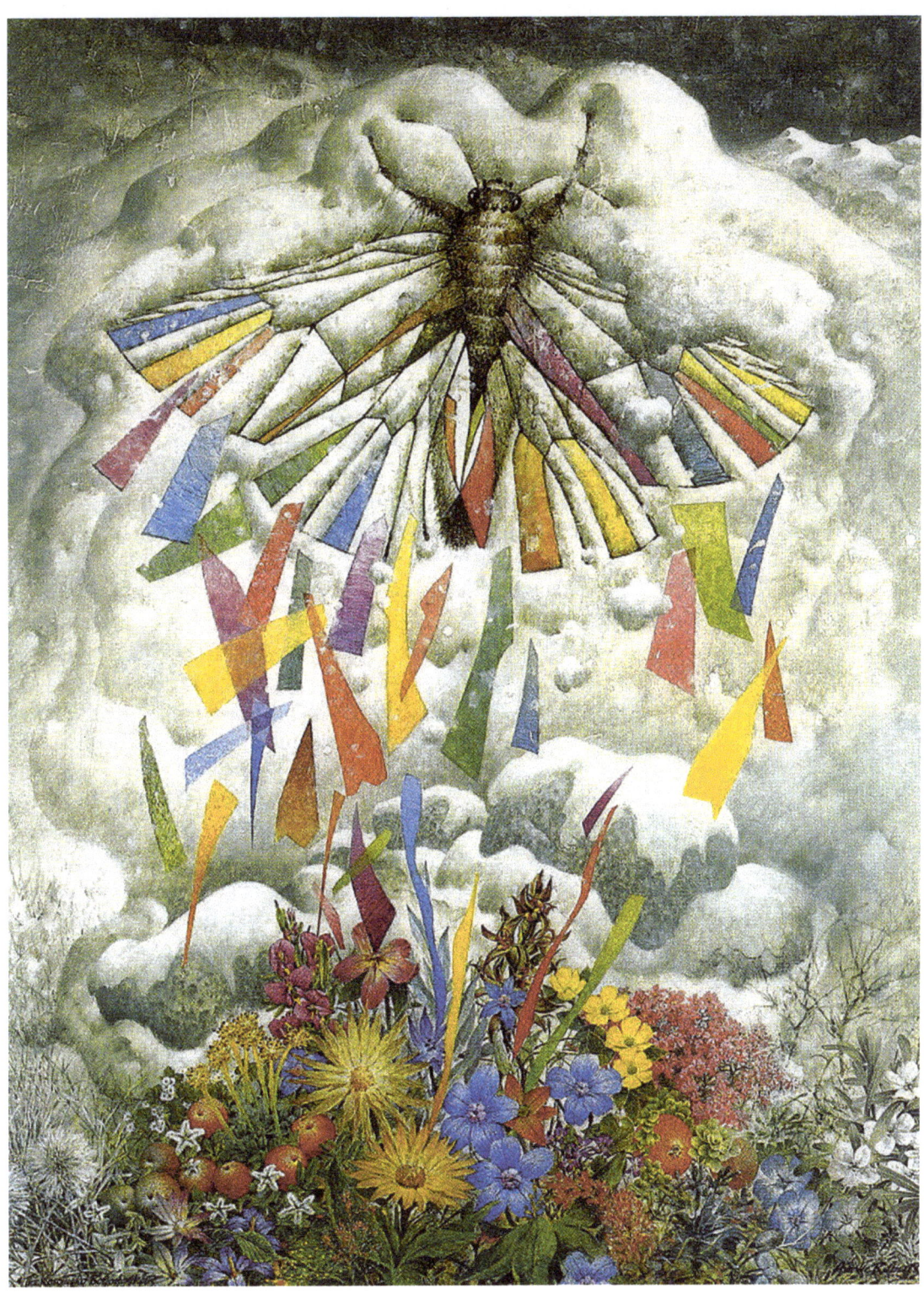

Mrs Melva Roberts

THE DESERT ICE-MEN

There would be few Australians today who are unfamiliar with The Weather Report. Expected maxima, isobars drawn on TV screen maps, high and low pressure cells - all are common jargon of our time. Because of it, we know when to wear extra clothing against the winter chills. The Aborigines of central Australia believe they know why.

For they accept that the Ninya ice-men are the creators of frost, ice and cold winds. They differ little in appearance from the Aborigines except that their bodies are covered with hoar-frost and their hair and whiskers are icicles.

The Ninya live in huge underground caverns. The walls are covered with ice and are swept constantly by howling cold winds. The only entrance to their home is on a low island in the Unagaltja salt lake. Close by are some boulders and stunted mulga trees.

During the hot summer months, the ice-men cluster happily together in their glacial home, but when winter comes, they roam the desert during the night, freezing the waterholes and leaving the ground covered with ice and frost.

Sometimes, should their return be delayed, the ice-men have to run to reach their underground caverns before the sun rises, knowing that its warmth would melt much of the ice on their bodies and so reduce their powers to create winter cold. On these occasions, their great rushing along creates the icy winds that sweep across the desert at dawn.

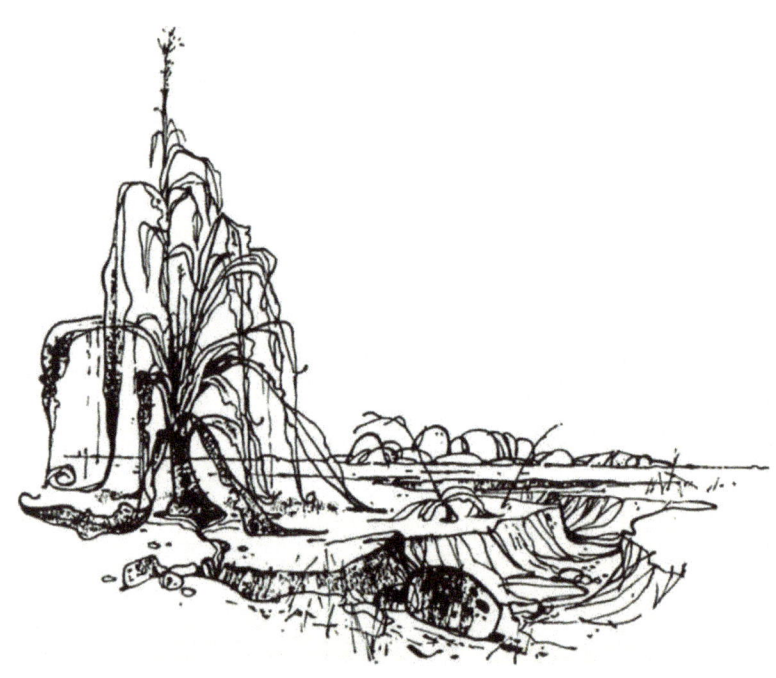

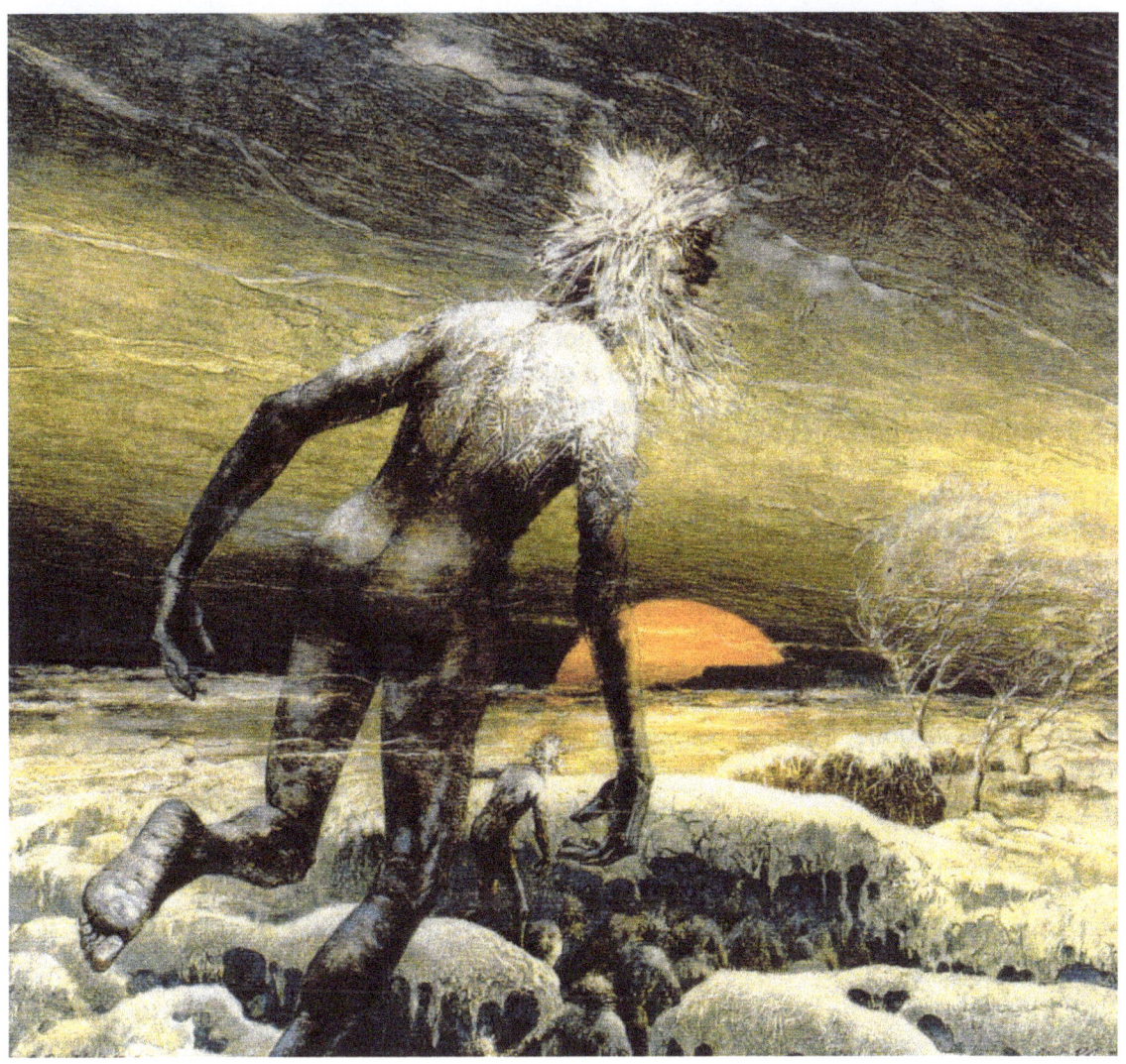

Mr and Mrs Charles E Hulley

TREES BORN OF FIRE

Children love stories. Often today their stories appear on TV screens instead of in picture books or at mother's knee. The presentation may change but the purpose of stories has always been both to entertain and to educate.

The moral of modern tales may not always be obviously stated. But Aboriginal stories are hundreds of centuries old. They are simple and direct with a very pointed message. One such story is this allegory of 'pride goes before a fall.'

Wapanga, although a great warrior, was unpopular. His preoccupation with his good looks and his arrogant attitude made the people of his tribe avoid him. Feeling outcast, he began to roam far from camp. One day he saw a young woman, Tilpana, in a neighbouring camp.

Wapanga was so captivated by her beauty that he returned many times until at last he found her alone. He asked her to go away with him, but Tilpana, liking him no better than did the women of his own tribe, made her feelings plain and ran back to her people.

Furious and humiliated, Wapanga was determined to have his revenge. On a day of fierce heat and high winds, he set light to the dense scrub near her camp. Soon a roaring bushfire swept down on the camp with such speed that few escaped alive.

Tilpana was one of the few who outran the fire. When she saw Wapanga standing in the ashes gloating over the dreadful carnage, she showed herself in the open. Wapanga ran after her. Tilpana lured him into a patch of thick scrub and waited. When Wapanga was almost upon her, she called on the spirits to help her and quickly surrounded him with a ring of flame and smoke.

As Wapanga tried to escape from his fiery prison, he saw with horror that seeds dropping from the trees around him burst into life as soon as they fell in the flames. They grew with such speed that he was instantly enclosed with a wall of growth so thick that he could not escape.

Exhausted, Wapanga fell into the flames and died. Tilpana, who had not managed her magic quickly enough to escape the fire of her own making, was badly burnt. As punishment for using forbidden secrets, she was transformed into the crow.

Ever since that time, the crow has been black, and the strongest seed germination in the Australian bush always follows a bushfire.

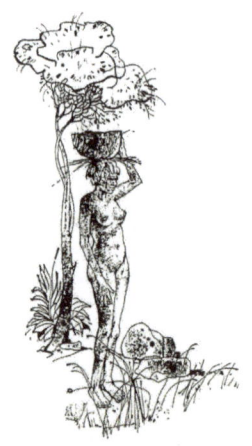

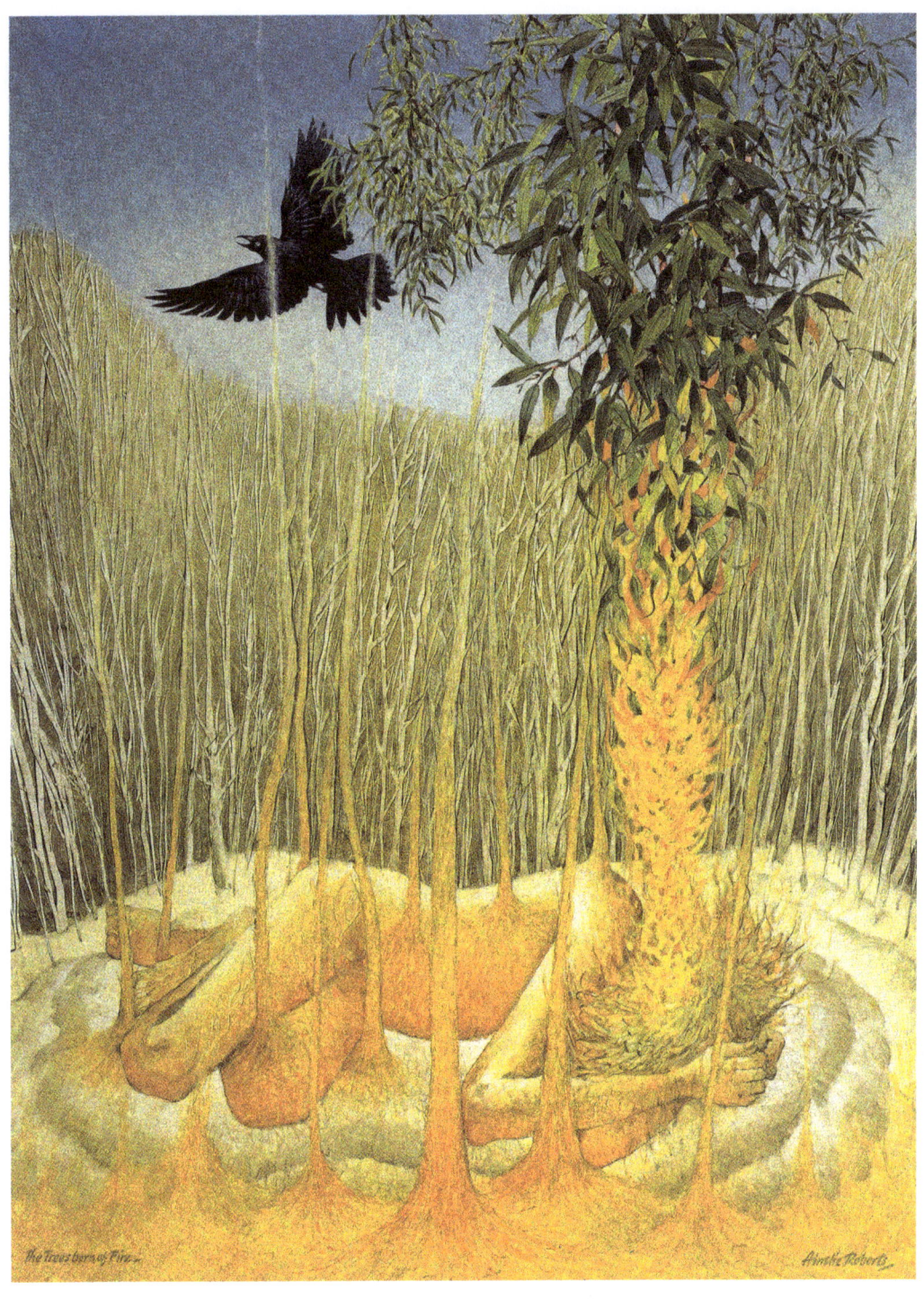

Mr Jack A Antonas

THE BURNING CORMORANT

The myths of their Dreamtime provide the Aborigines with a logical explanation for the world in which they live - why there is a mountain here or there, why the sun rises each day, why the wind blows coldly across the desert, even why birds are specific colours.

The Aborigines of Yorke Peninsula in South Australia believe that the cormorant or shag originated in this way, long ago in the Dreamtime.

Buthera, a powerful tribal elder, was on a journey to visit a distant southern tribe when he encountered an old enemy, Madjitju. Buthera accused Madjitju of trespassing and, after exchanging many insults, they resorted to violence. They fought for many hours until finally Madjitju suffered so many injuries that he died.

Exhausted and in pain, Buthera slowly continued his journey and at last reached his destination. But he was angry to find that the willy-wagtail, always the first with any news - and always the first to gossip about it - had spread stories of the fight far and wide. Not only did the whole tribe know about the fight and Madjitju's death, but some of the many variations of the story were plainly damaging to Buthera's prestige.

Now Buthera was a renowned man of magic as well as a great chief, so he used his magical powers to punish the tribe for spreading malicious gossip about him. He pointed his spear to the east, to the south, to the west and finally to the north.

Fires sprang up everywhere and a great wind came down from the north. Soon the whole country was blazing, and the tribe crowded into the deep waterholes to escape the flames. Having burnt out their country, Buthera finally took pity on them and transformed all of them into cormorants. To this day, the cormorant has white only underneath. The rest of him is jet-black where he was scorched by Buthera's fire. The willy-wagtail, who was also caught in the fire, is marked in the same way. And he is still an inquisitive gossiper.

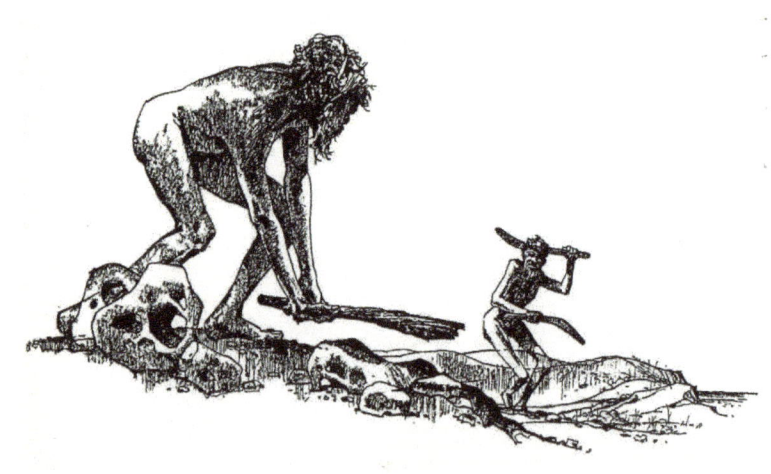

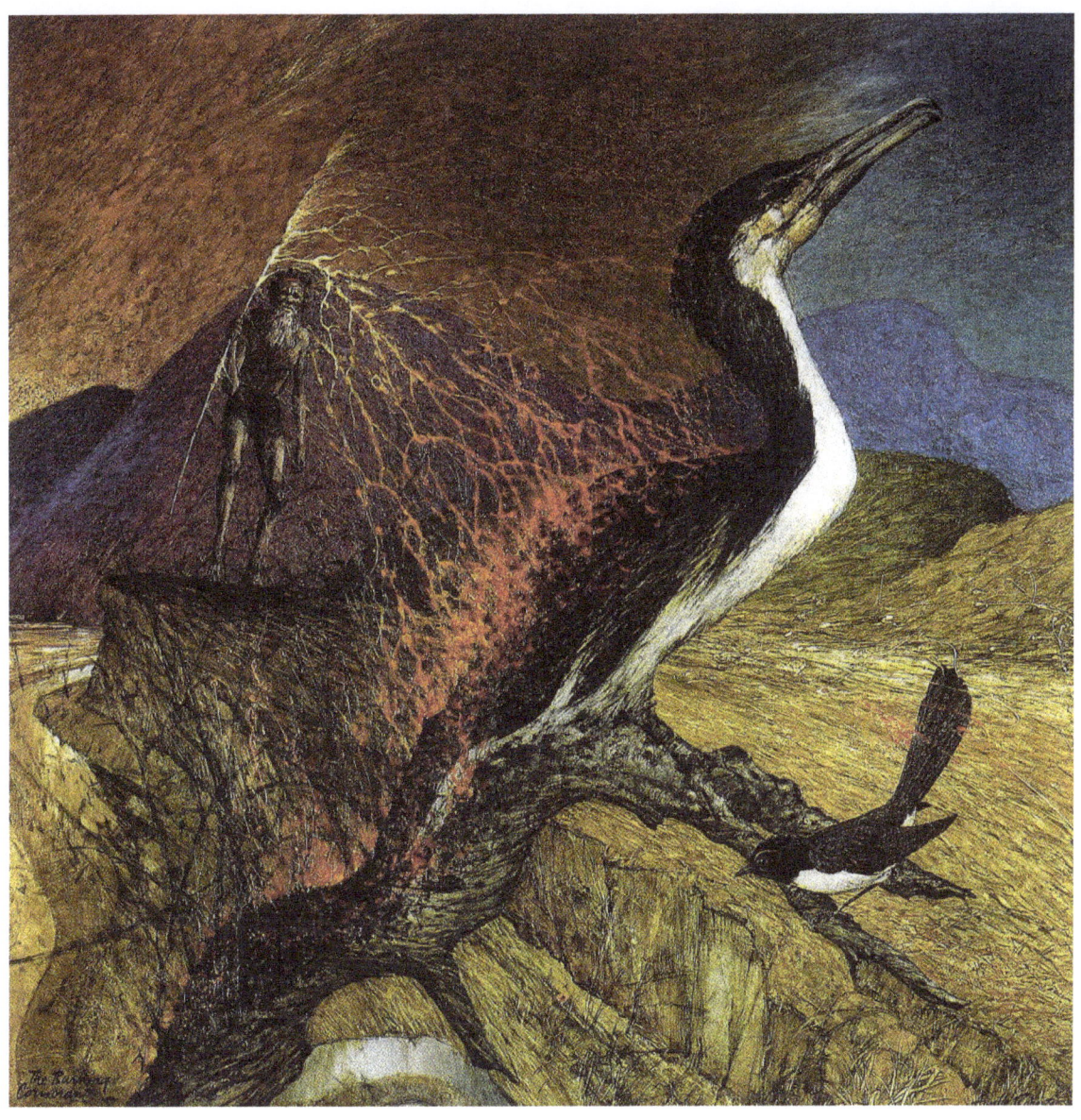

Mr and Mrs Rhys Roberts

BIRTH OF THE OPAL

Australia is the eighth wonder of the world. A lifetime is not long enough to explore all its natural beauties. So often we are limited to brief holidays at the main 'tourist attractions'. And, of course, we take home memories and gifts in the form of souvenirs.

Opal is a typically Australian souvenir. This Aboriginal story tells of its origins.

In the Andamooka area, the Dreamtime creator came down to earth on a great rainbow. He gathered his tribes together and instructed them on the laws they were to follow and established their way of life.

He told them that he would return when he judged they were wise enough to carry out his plan for unending peace on earth. They would know when that time had come by the rainbow which would appear in the sky. It would be so much bigger and brighter and so different in shape from the usual rainbow that they could not mistake it.

When the creator had finished speaking, the rainbow bore him back to the sky. Where the rainbow had rested, there was now a great area of rocks and pebbles that flashed and glittered in the sun with all the colours of the rainbow that had given them birth - red, orange, green, blue, yellow, indigo and violet. These were the first opals.

From that time on, the Aborigines believed that their creator would again appear at that spot and regarded the area as sacred.

In other opal-bearing areas of Australia, opals were looked upon merely as pretty stones. But in the Andamooka region, the opal was sacred because of its mystical association with the creator and the great rainbow in which he would one day reappear.

Today, the opal is still a precious object but only in the sense of commercial gain. Under the impact of European influence, the once-hallowed spot has become a market place for white men and the Aborigines alike.

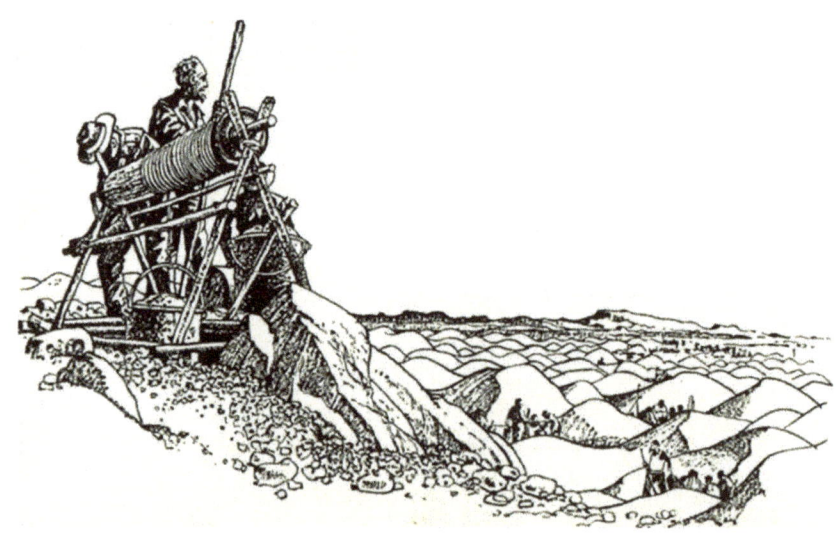

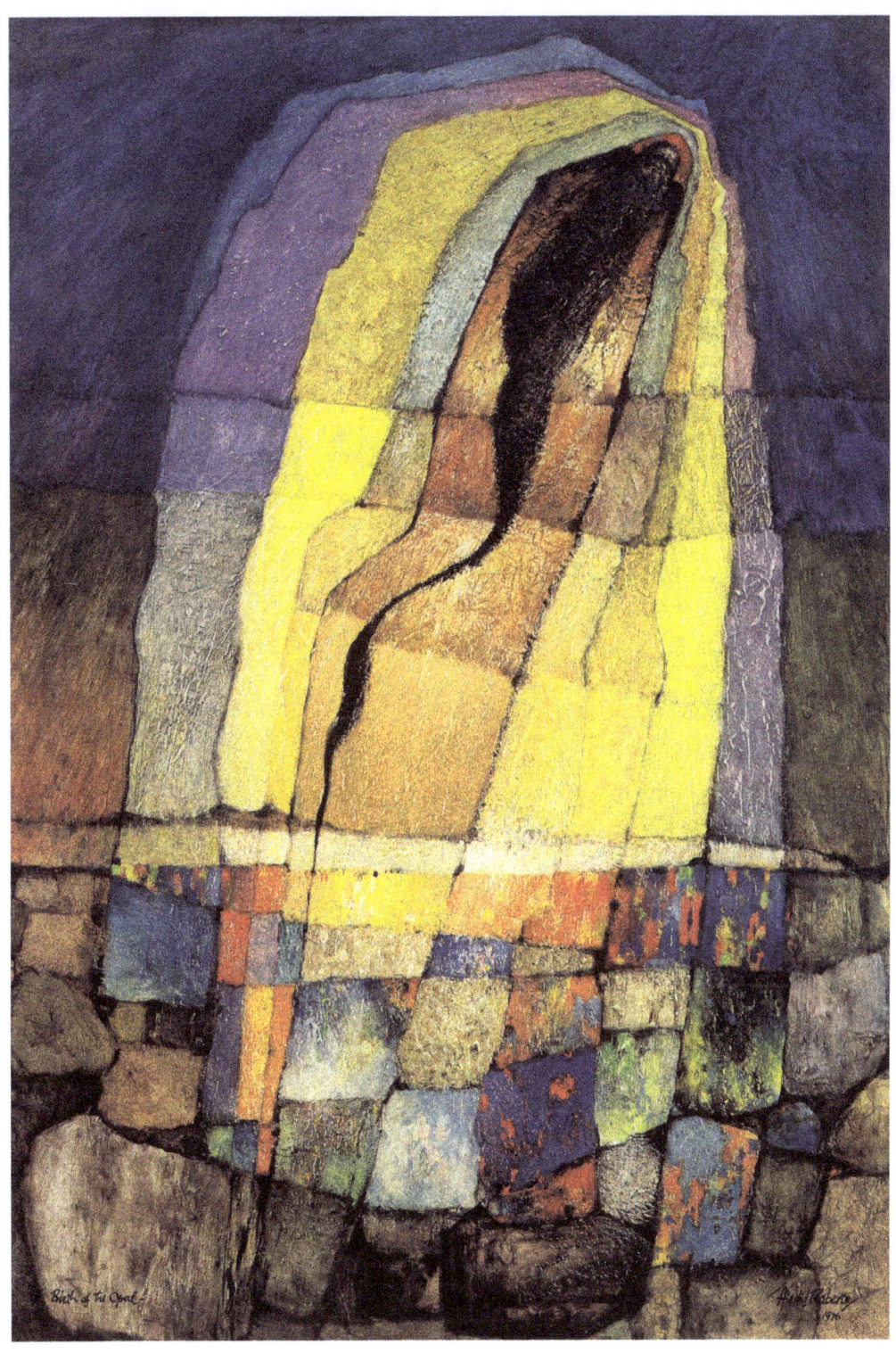

Mrs M J Roberts

THE GUARDIAN OF OWL ROCK

Australia is an ancient land, undisturbed by any major geological upheavals for millions of years. Its topography boasts many strange rocky features found nowhere else: Ayers Rock, the largest single rock in the world; the Devil's Marbles; the Glass House Mountains.

The Aborigines have an explanation for all these natural phenomena, an explanation that derives from some happening in the Dreamtime.

One such phenomenon is Owl Rock in Pulkakurinya Gorge, three hundred kilometres north-west of Alice Springs. It stands guard over the only permanent waterhole in this remote area.

In the Dreamtime days of the Aborigines of central Australia, Buk-Buk the owl and his two wives came to this spot in search of water. Drought had driven them from the Bigili rockhole to the north.

Determined never to be forced to search for water again, Buk-Buk has ever since stood guard over this waterhole - which has never been known to dry up. And there at its entrance today looms Owl Rock, testimony to that guardianship.

This unique and unexplained wedge-like stone rises to a height of more than ten metres and, although it is up to four metres thick, it balances on a base barely a metre in diameter. Its vertical strata stand out in marked contrast to the horizontal layering of all the surrounding hills-an everlasting puzzle to modern geologists.

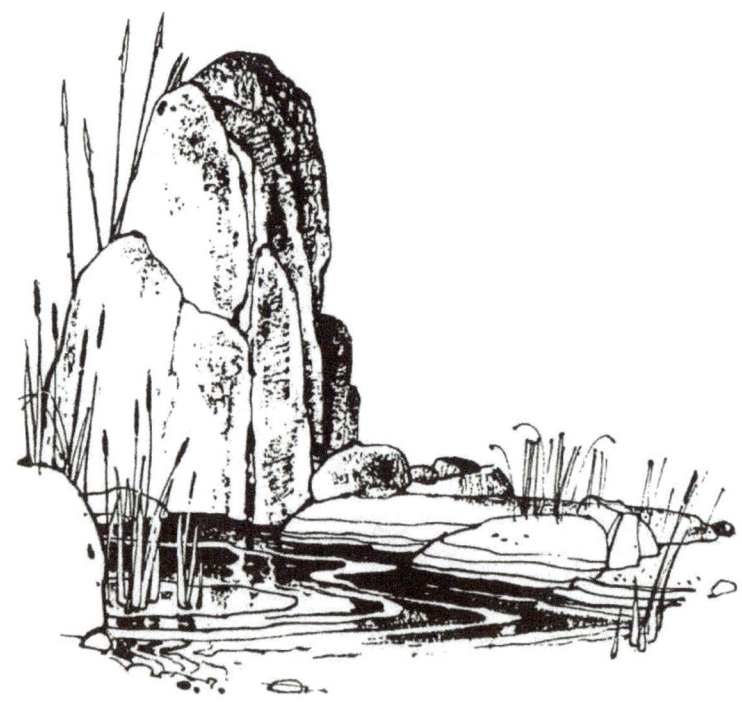

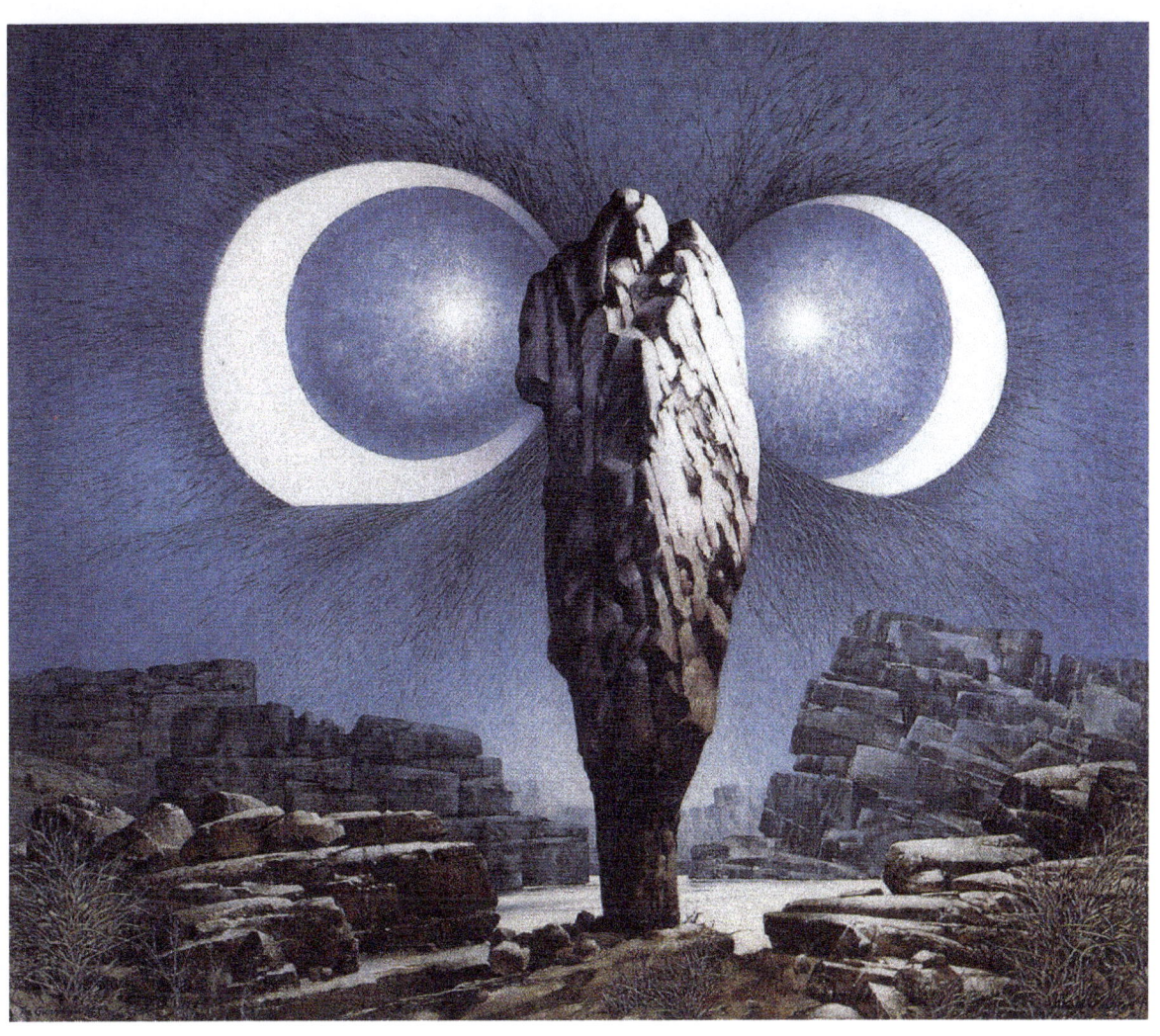

Mr and Mrs Charles E Hulley

BIRTHPLACE OF THE MOONS

For centuries, astronomers, lyricists and romantics alike have been inspired by the miracle of the moon. Its constant waxing and waning have, since time began, induced fear or fascination in the hearts and minds of mankind.

The Aborigines, too, have stories to explain its mystery. Their mythology records that in the earliest days of the Dreamtime, the moon did not wax or wane but shone constantly as a full moon. But it was always misbehaving. So as a punishment for its indiscretions, the spirits decreed that each month the moon must die for three days.

A variation of this myth describes how full moons were born and how they waned.

There was once a place known as the Valley of the Moons where the soil was the richest on earth and in it grew the moons. When each moon had grown large enough to leave the valley and venture up into the night sky, it would break free of its mother plant and float about in the valley until its turn came to take its place in the heavens.

Like most living things, the moons needed the sun in order to grow big and strong. But the sun was really their enemy because it was jealous of anything that tried to share the sky with it.

So when each moon rose out of the valley each month, the sun - huge, hot and powerful - would race across the sky in pursuit and reach out with its fiery fingers to tear pieces off the moon until it was all gone. The tiny pieces that broke free when this happened became the stars.

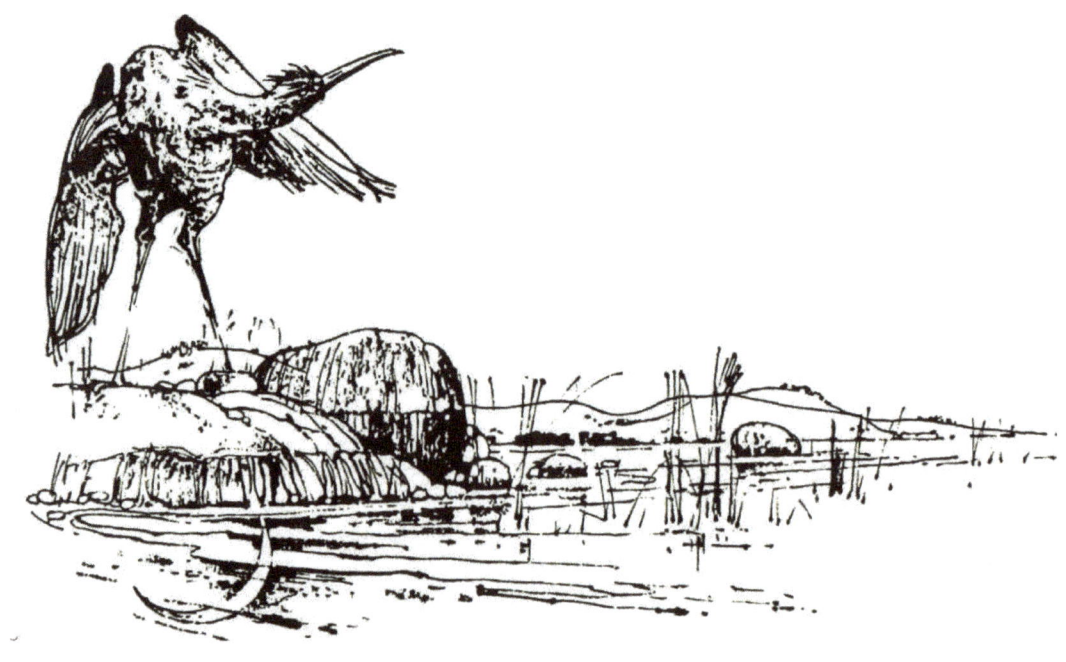

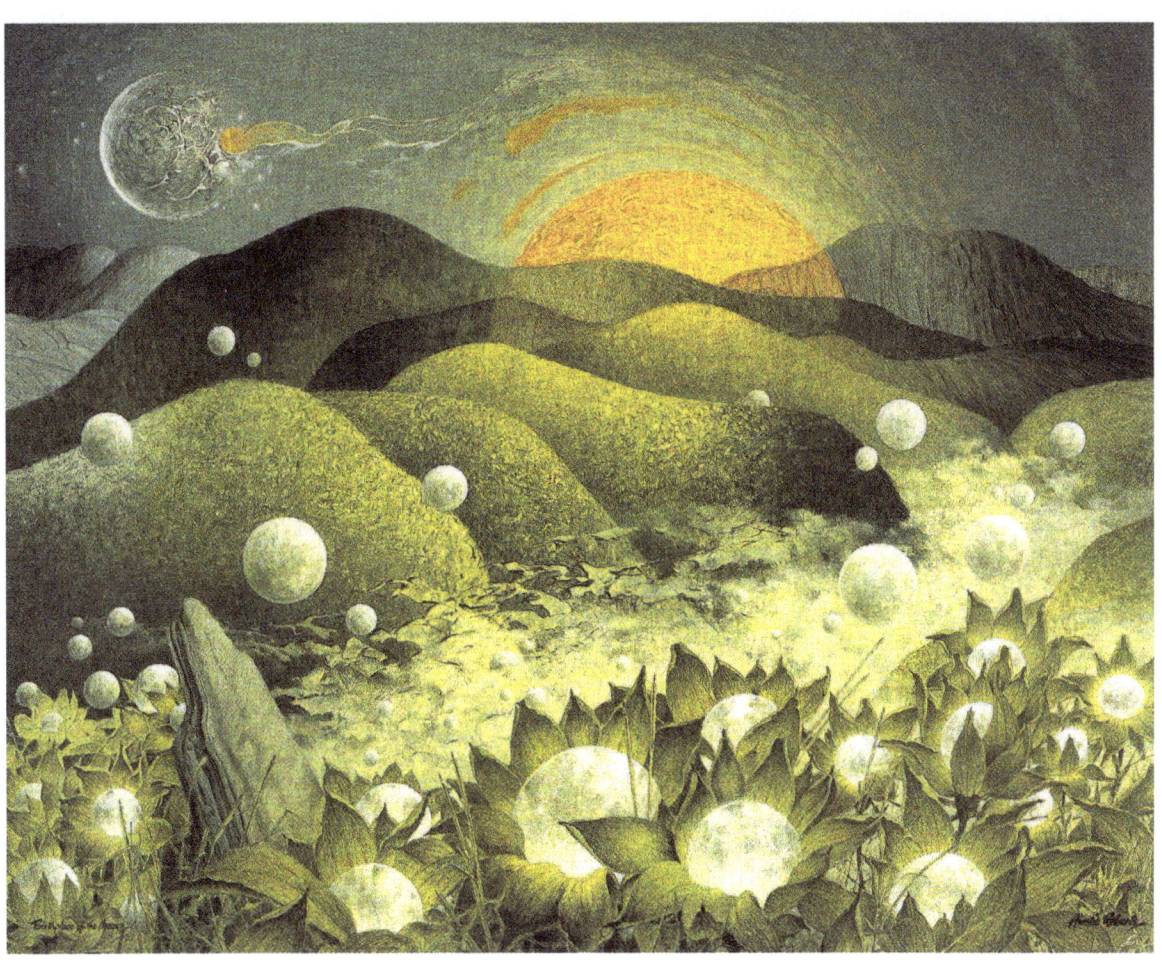

Mr Steve Carapetis

THE SEARCH FOR MOODAI

Zoologists tell us that it is a natural law that function governs structure. Hence evolution endowed the platypus with a bill remarkably adapted for its semi-amphibious existence; or the camel with perfect sand-shoes; or the whale with great paddles for arms.

Aboriginal explanations of animal appearance or behaviour are far less mundane. The myths from their Dreamtime provide them with simple solutions to questions scientists have puzzled over for centuries.

One such story from the Flinders Ranges tells of Moodai, the possum-man. He was a mighty hunter who kept not only his own but also many other families of his tribe well supplied with food.

On his hunting trips he often took his two small sons. They were always asking Moodai to tell them more about the great moon that sometimes hung overhead in the starlit sky.

He told them the stories of how the moon grows and how it is eaten away by the sun which chases it across the heavens each month. The boys' fascination with the moon deepened.

One bright evening when the moon was full and they were out hunting, Moodai saw a very tall thin tree that looked likely to yield a good meal of witchetty grubs. Instructing his sons to hold the trunk of the tree steady, Moodai began to climb up and up. When he reached the very top, he called out to the boys that he could touch the moon. In their excitement, they let go of the tree which began to bend and fall as its roots were torn from the ground.

Moodai jumped to the moon for safety as the great tree fell to earth. The two boys frantically climbed every tree they could to try to reach their father in the moon, but none was tall enough.

Ever since then, especially at the time of full moon, the boys and other possums from the tribe can still be seen climbing the tallest trees in an endless search for the great hunter. Moodai still looks down on his own sons who are now the rare albino possums. They are the colour of the cold night moon - a special reminder of the fate of their father.

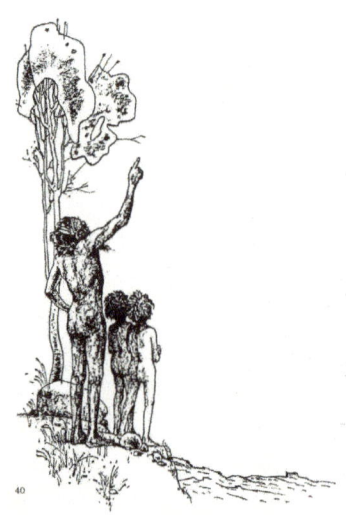

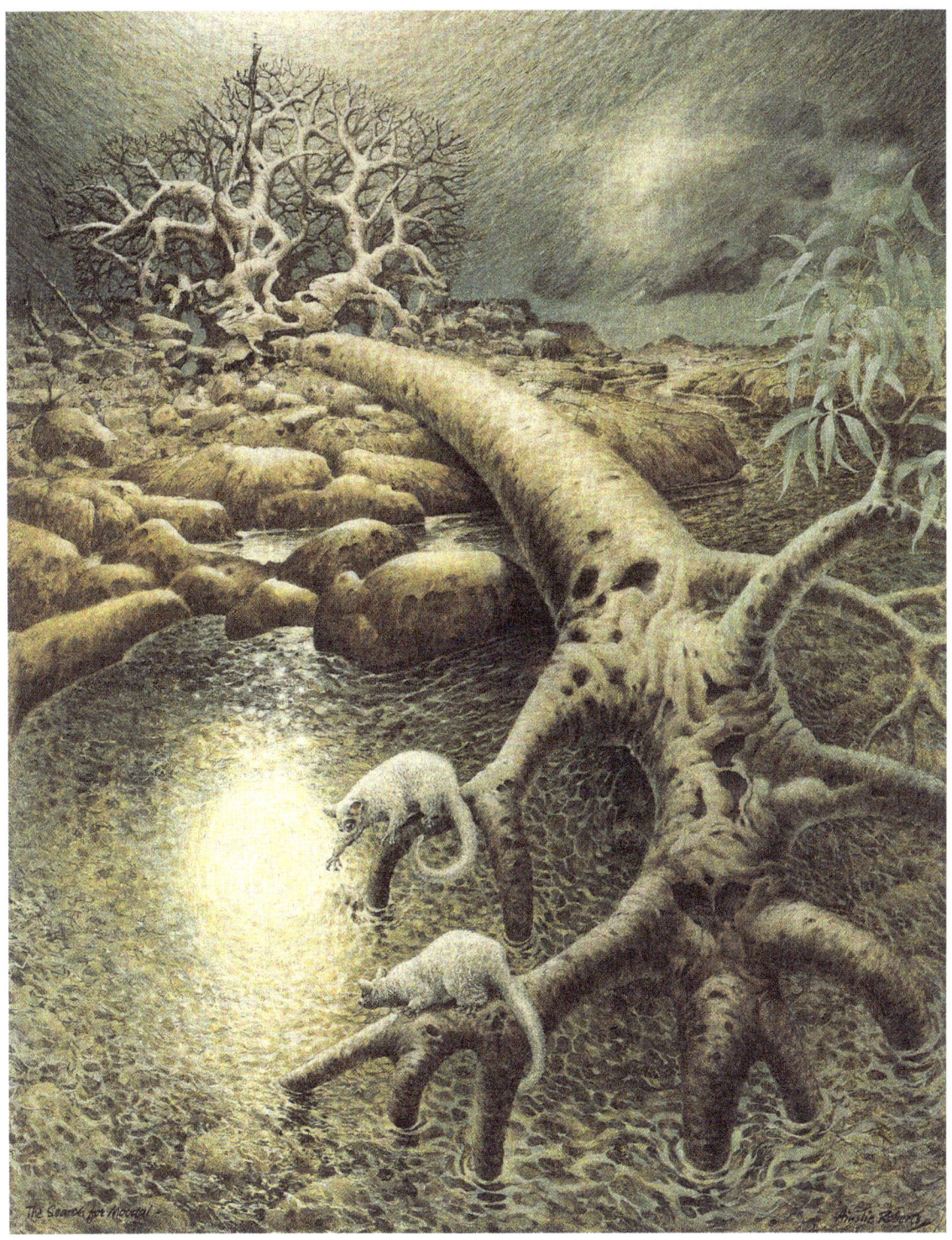

Private Collection

WIRA REBORN

Aboriginal Dreamtime myths often vary from tribe to tribe. This version of the story of the creation of the moon is from the Wongaibon Tribe.

It was once the duty of a lazy and bad-tempered moon-man, Wira, to train his two nephews in the ways of the tribe. When they became efficient hunters and skilled in the magic which he taught them, he spent most of his time resting and ordering them to feed him.

Eventually the two brothers became so angry at this dictatorial behaviour that they planned to rid themselves of his domination. They knew that his favourite food was the wood grubs that live high in the gum trees. But tribal law forbade young men to take the grubs from the trees.

So one day they ran to him and said that they had found a tree rich with the grubs. In great excitement, Wira followed them to the tree and climbed up. When he was high in the branches, they used the magic he had taught them to make the tree grow higher.

It grew so high and so fast that Wira soon found to his astonishment that he was high enough to touch the sky. He hooked his fingers curiously into the sky to discover what it felt like. Instantly the nephews brought the tree down to its normal size. Wira was left hanging from the sky.

The nephews called up to him, "We've put you up there to punish you for your laziness and bad temper. Each month you will become sick and thin and come down into the mountains to die. Then, after three days, you will be reborn and go up into the sky again to grow large and fat, then come down to die again. And that will happen to you for ever and ever."

But the triumph of the nephews was short-lived. The new moon-man called up his own powerful magic and changed them into stars and placed them in the sky. For ever afterwards they have had to live there, still close to their lazy uncle.

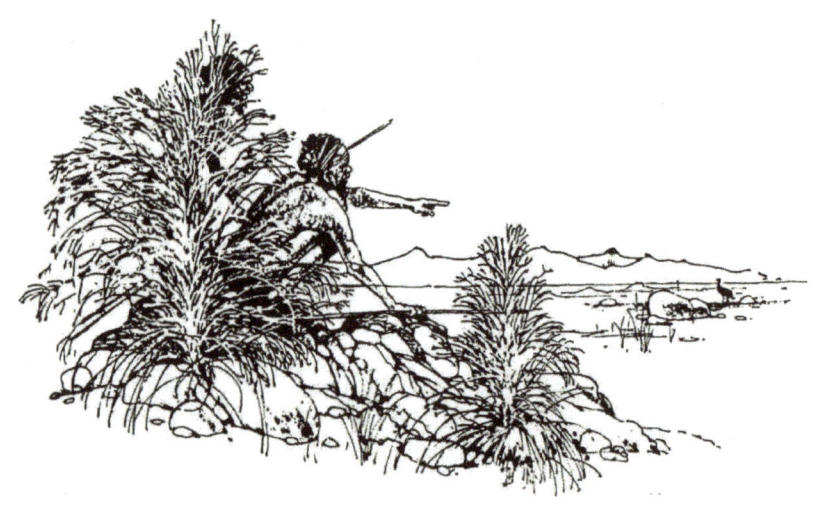

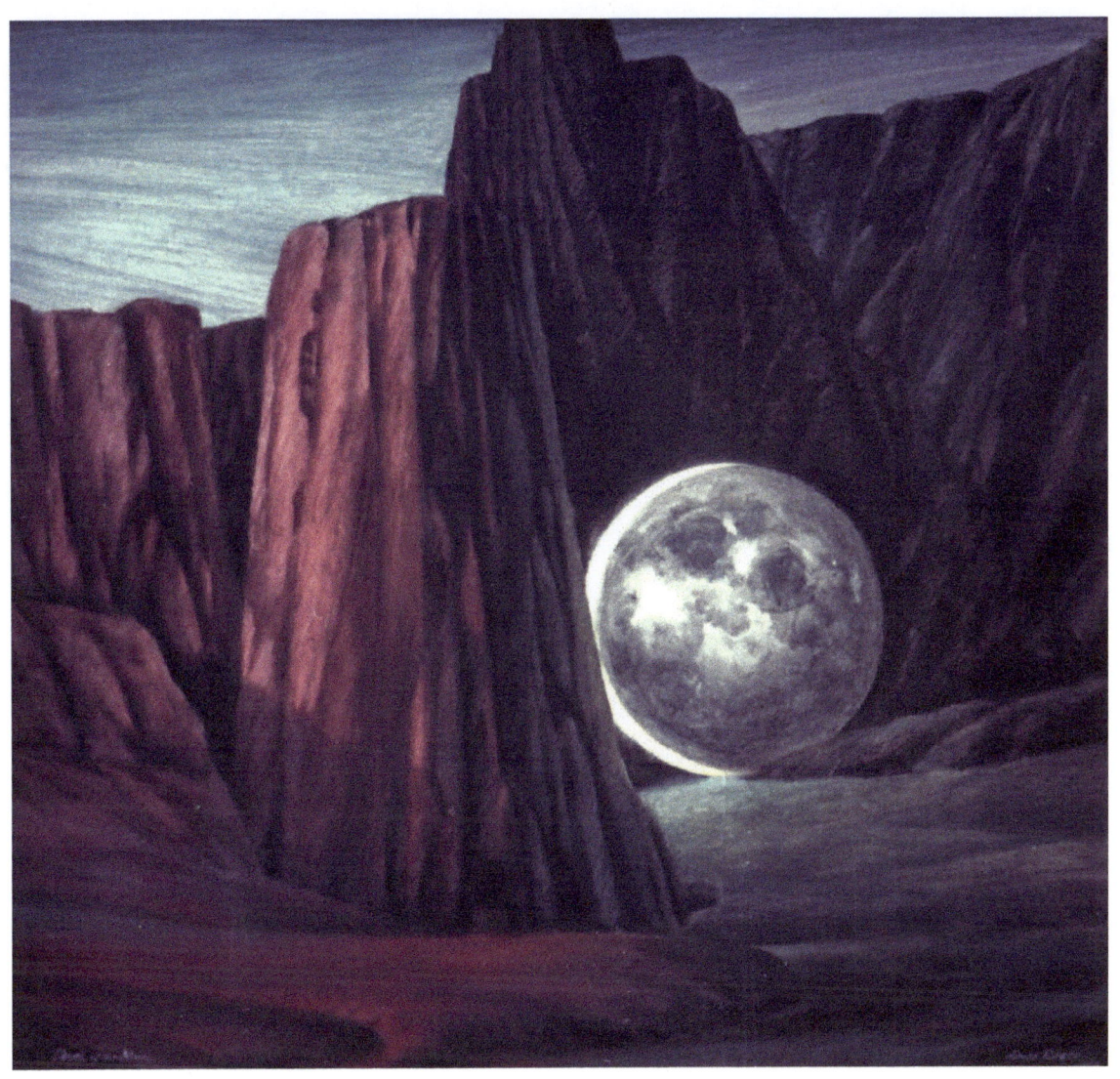

Mr and Mrs Charles E Hulley

WUNGALA AND THE EVIL-BIG-EYED-ONE

Children the world over have always been warned of the consequences of their misdeeds. Avenging ghosts and goblins, bad fairies and evil monsters are all part of the dark corners of children's minds. This is the Aboriginal version of 'the bogie-man will get you if you're not good'.

Wungala was away from the camp with her small son, Bulla. They had been gathering seeds all morning. Afterwards, she sat at her milling stone and ground the seeds into powder, then added water to make it into a thick dough. Bulla ran around, laughing and talking to himself.

The sun shone brightly at first, but when some clouds threw a shadow across the earth, Wungala called her son to her and told him to stay close, warning him that he must now remain quiet. When Bulla asked why, his mother explained

that with the shadows came the Evil-Big-Eyed-One from his cave in the hills and, should it hear Bulla's chattering, it would seek him out and them both up.

Bulla, being very small and forgetful, wandered off again, only to rush back to his mother screaming that he had seen the evil one. Wungala, too, had seen it coming their way but she said, "You are wrong, Bulla. Nothing is there but the shadows made by some waving bushes."

She spoke as calmly as she could, knowing that they were safe only if she pretended that the evil one was not there. So she went on talking calmly, making more and more dough and finally putting it on the hot coals to bake.

Each time the Evil-Big-Eyed-One came closer and roared at them, Bulla cried out in fear. And each time Wungala calmed Bulla by telling him that the noise was only some small animal.

The evil creature was puzzled and wondered why it seemed to be invisible to the woman. In its curiosity, it crept up behind her. Wungala gathered up the dough in both hands, swung around and threw the hot sticky mass in its face.

Quickly picking up her son, Wungala fled back to the camp and the safety of her people, leaving the evil-one roaring in agony as it tried to scrape the hot dough from its eye and mouth.

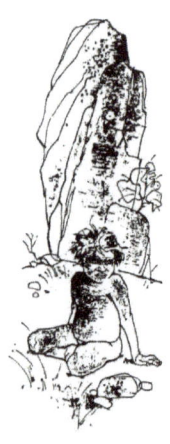

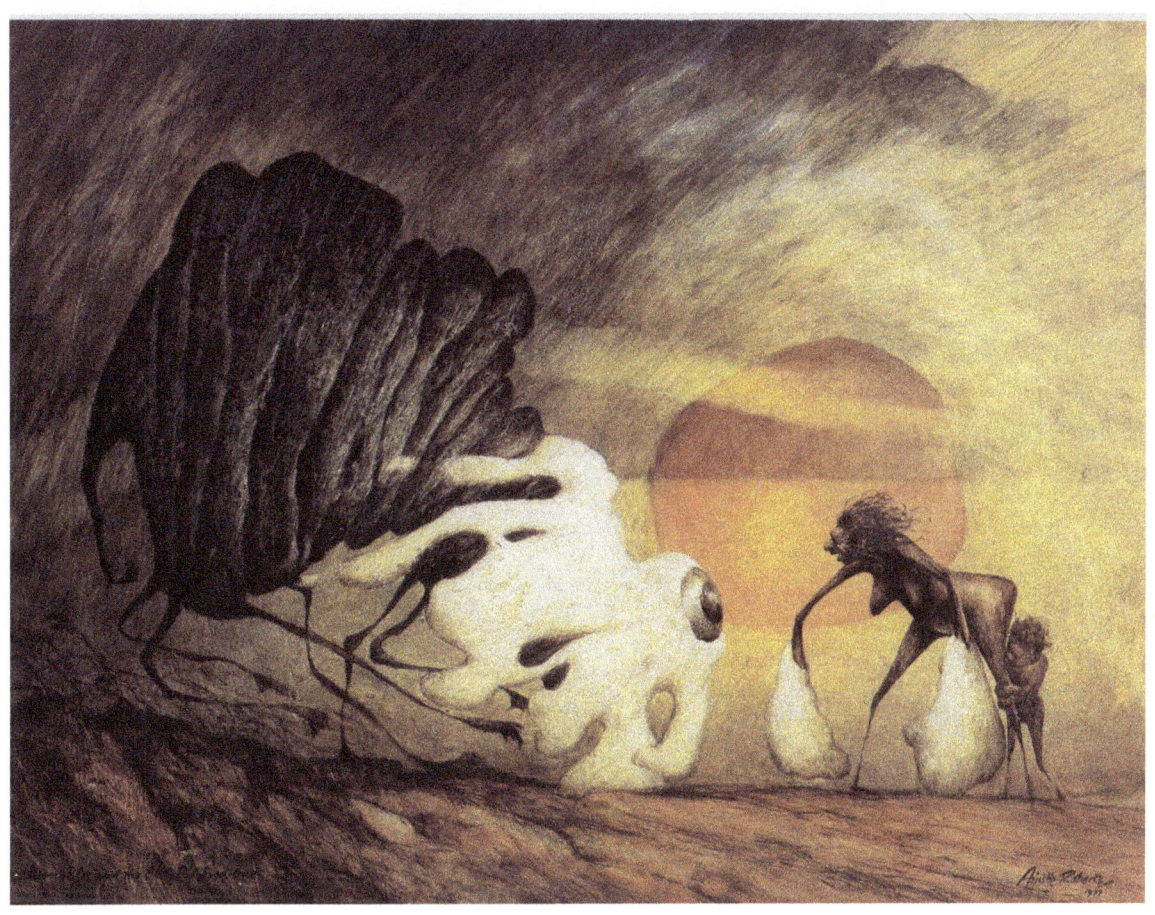

Mr Fraser Hay

EERIN THE PROTECTOR

To the modern child, an owl is a bird which hoots. To the ornithologist, it is the order Strigiformes. To the Aborigines, it is a signal.

Indeed, Australian Aborigines have an uncanny sense of approaching danger. They read the sights and sounds of their environment as a jet pilot reads his radar screen.

For once in the Dream time there lived a man called Eerin. He was not strong nor particularly brave. He was a poor hunter and contributed little to the life of his tribe, except for one special quality.

Eerin had exceptionally keen hearing and was a very light sleeper. If an enemy tried to steal into the camp at night, there was no chance of his being, able to do so. For before he could get close enough to use his weapons, Eerin would cry out 'Mil! Mil!' meaning 'Look out! Look out!'

Eerin lived to a great age and was much loved by his tribe, for even when he was old and frail, he could still be relied on to protect his tribe at night.

When he died, his tribe honoured his memory with a great corroboree and lit many fires. Yet even while they were still grieving, the neighbouring emu tribe tried to take advantage of their sorrow by attacking at night.

Again the tribe was saved by the familiar warning cry of 'Mil! Mil!' They searched to see who could have warned them now they no longer had their protector. And in the smoke they saw the spirit of Eerin in the form of a small owl.

Eerin, the grey owl, still rests by day. And at night, he hovers above his sleeping companions, ready to warn them whenever danger threatens.

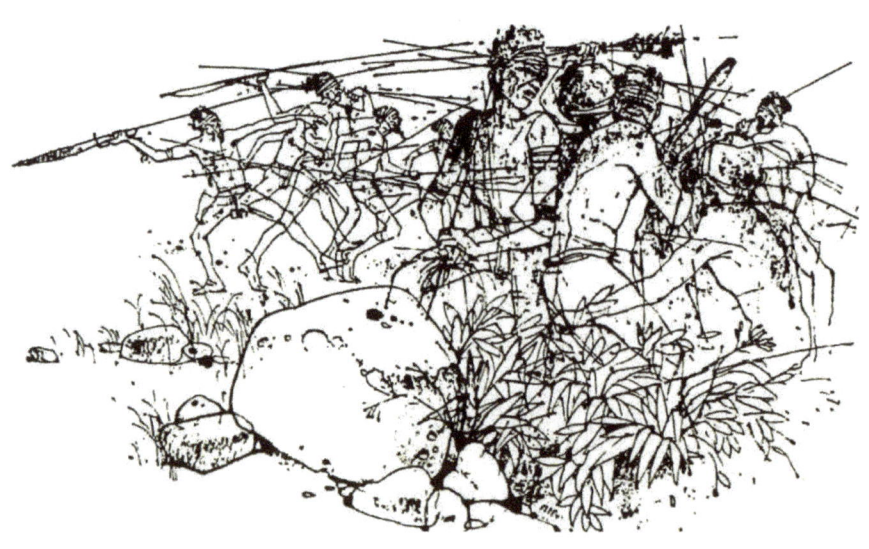

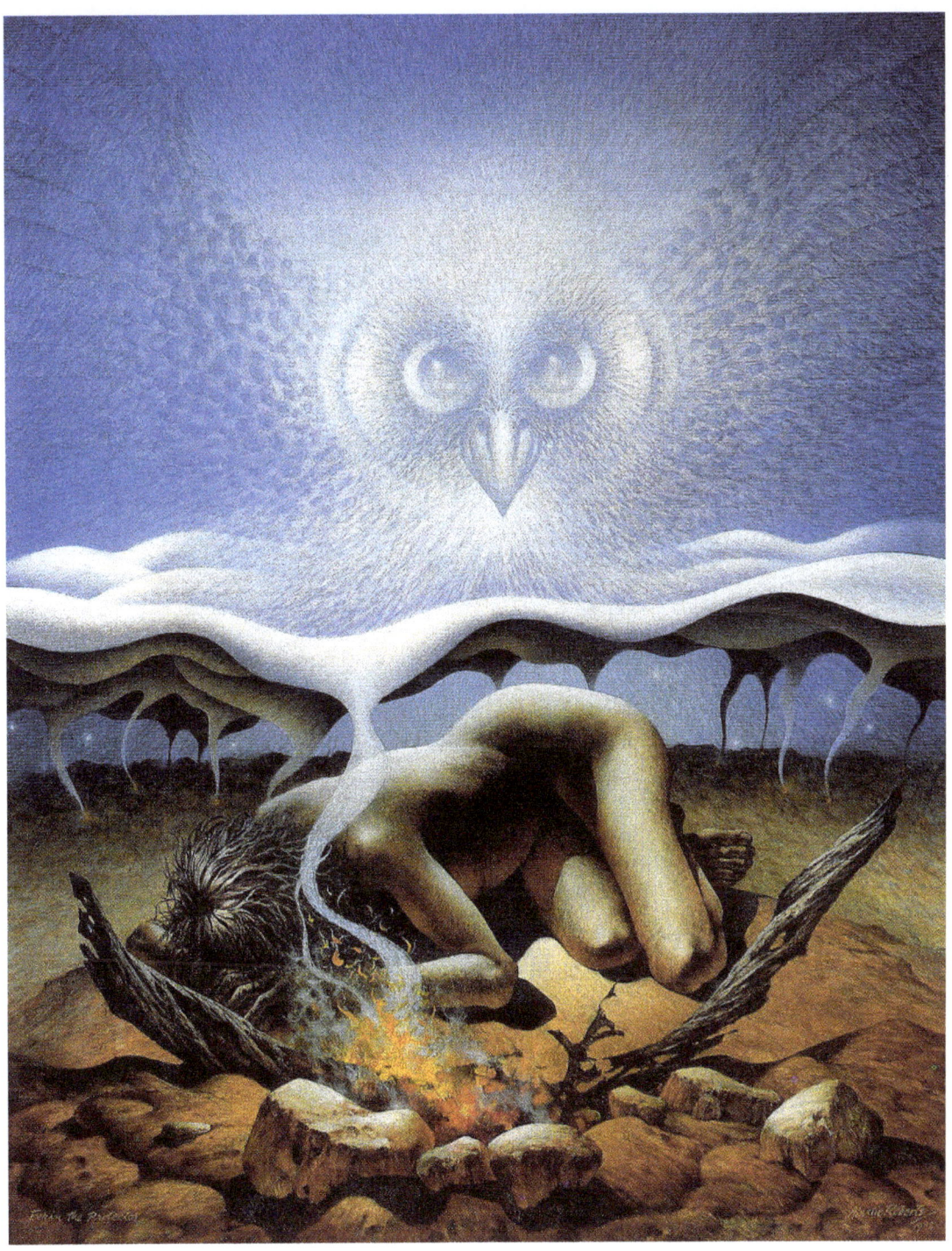

Helen Boyd Collection

STORM WARNING

The stars in the sky, too, provide the Aborigines with warning signals, as this myth relates.

Once there were two brothers, Nuruguya and Napiranbiru, who were very good fishermen. One day the brothers were catching so many fish that they did not notice the gathering storm clouds. Only a sudden roll of thunder made them look up. To their dismay they saw a curtain of slanting rain racing towards them across the water.

The brothers paddled swiftly for the shore but the rain caught them, pouring down in blinding sheets which filled their canoe faster than they could empty it with their bailer shell. Finally, the power of the wind, the huge waves and the weight of the water in it broke the canoe. Suddenly the brothers were swimming in the wild water.

Nuruguya was a stronger swimmer than his younger brother and he pushed his paddle, which he still had, under his brother's arm. As they swam side by side, the elder brother felt even his great strength leaving him and he let his younger brother swim ahead of him.

The storm stopped as suddenly as it had begun. Napiranbiru on his paddle got close enough to the shore to be rescued by the men of his tribe. But there was no sign of Nuruguya. Instead, as night came, the people saw a bright new star shining above their camp. "It is Nuruguya the elder brother," they said.

When the time came for Napiranbiru to die after a long life, he asked the spirits to let him join his brother as a star. They can still be seen there today in the Milky Way.

And when bad weather is brewing, especially as unexpected a storm as caught the brothers long ago, they come down from the sky with their canoe to the sea where they used to fish so happily. They appear as two great stars - a storm warning from the brothers who are the spirit guardians of the men who go out to fish in their little canoes.

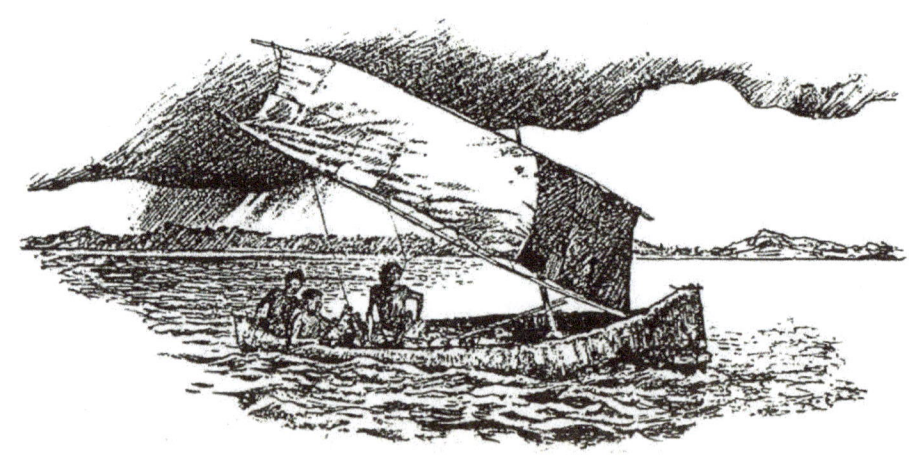

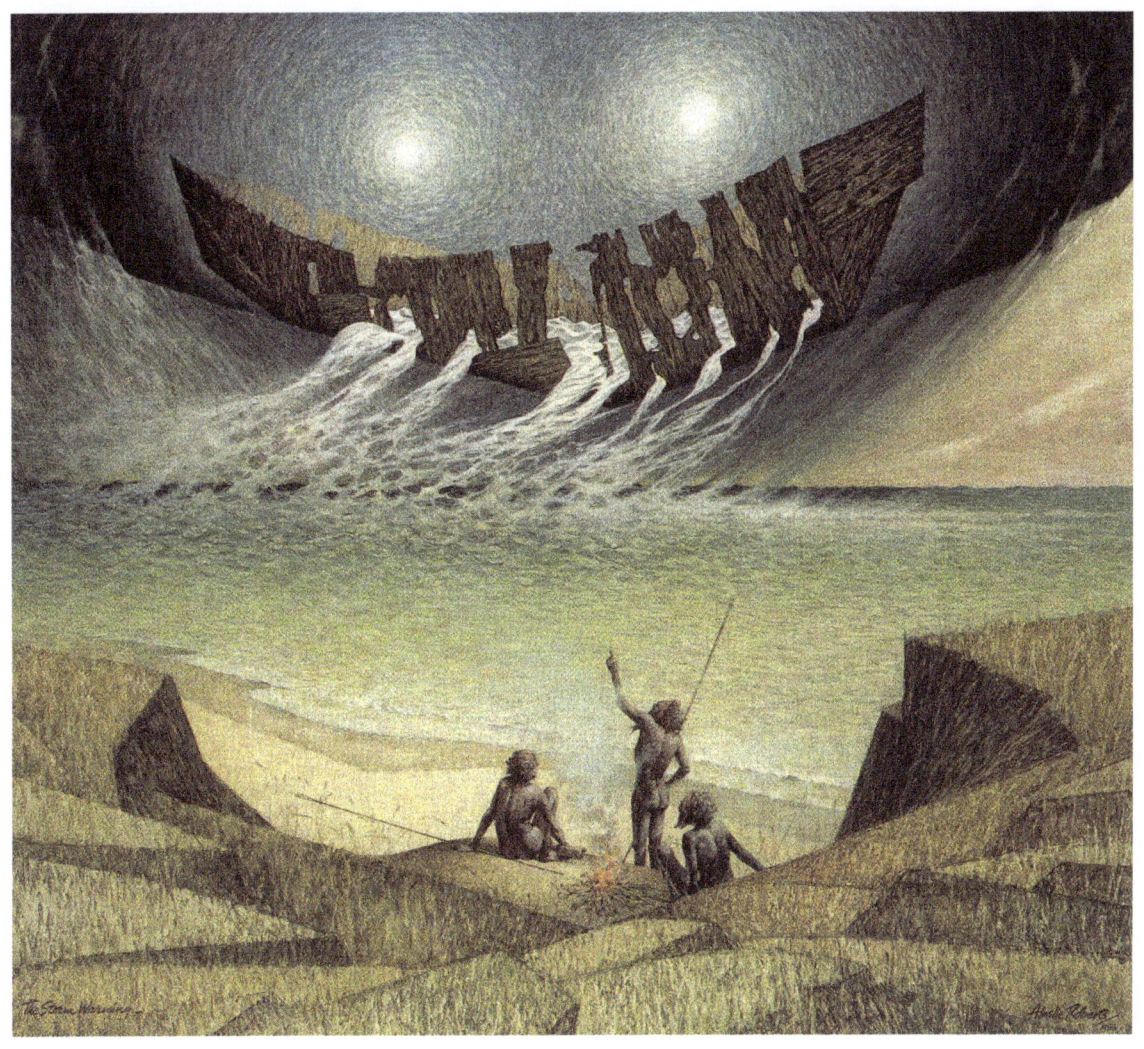

Mr Ted Norman

KALALA THE FIRE-TAILED FINCH

All cultures have their heroes. There are modern ones in football jumpers; there are heroes in stories from the past. David defeated Goliath with his sling-shot. Today the Davids use sporting equipment.

Aboriginal mythology, too, abounds in heroes. One was Kalala. His legend begins in the time when the tribes had possessed fire for so long that they had forgotten how to make it. When two evil spirits (in the form of hideous old women) appeared on earth and stole every fire, the people were cold and miserable.

The warriors made many brave attempts to storm the camp of the two women, but they had surrounded it by such a powerful spell that even the medicine men were powerless to break through. But Kalala, a small crippled man, shrewdly reasoned that the two evil women would not consider a person so small and deformed as he would be a threat to them.

So after many months of patiently doing useful tasks around the women's camp, they allowed him insicle the magic circle. Kalala, knowing that even one piece of wood taken from the camp fire would deprive the women of all their magic powers, bided his time. Then one night he snatched a burning stick from their fire and fled into the darkness.

Screaming with rage, the women set off after him, following the red pin-point of light. The chase continued until he was dying from exhaustion and was almost within reach of camp.

With the torch almost burnt away, he used the last of his strength and courage to cup his hands around the tell-tale flame and lie down on it. As he died, he heard the evil ones blunder past him and on to the waiting spears of his tribesmen.

Where Kalala's body had been, his people found a small bird guarding the last live coals of his fire-stick. From that time on, the fire-tailed finch was revered, for it held the spirit of Kalala, the cripple who brought fire back to the Aborigines.

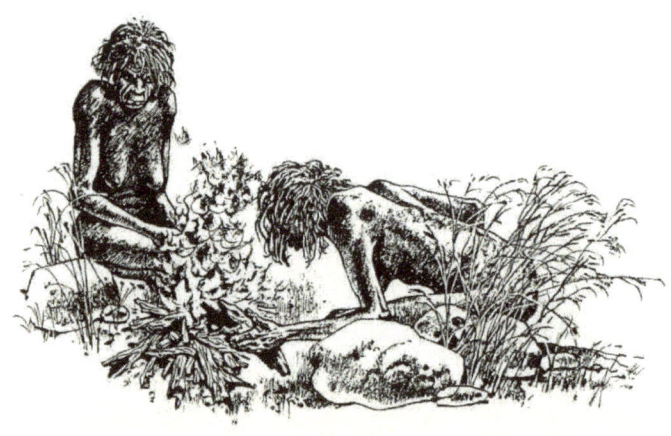

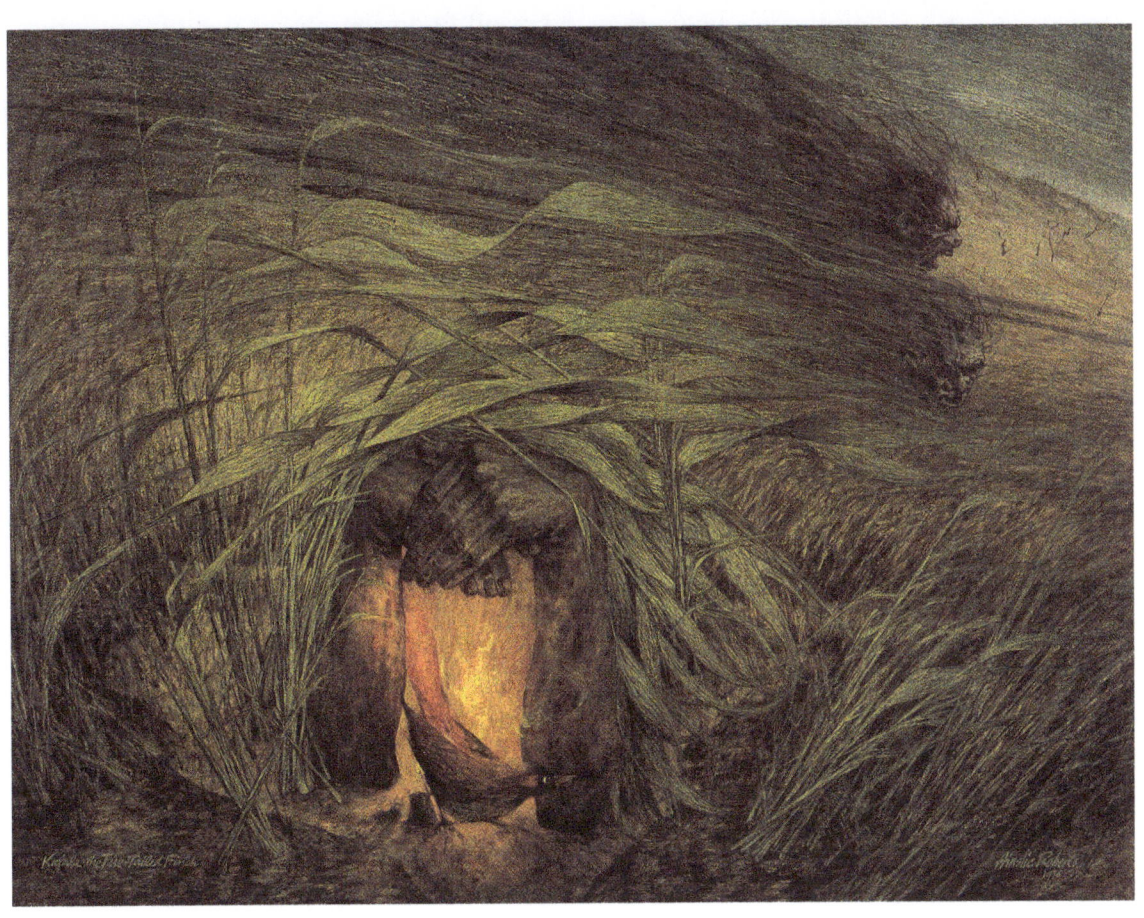

Mr Samuel and Mrs Wendy Olenik

THE RAIN DRAGON

How often have we heard of foolhardy travellers lost in the Australian outback? And so frequently when they are found, they have no water.

But the Australian Aborigines have adapted their lives to prosper in the driest parts of the driest continent on earth. Their proven ability to survive and find water under the most arduous of conditions is awesome.

It is not surprising that in this harsh land of repeated droughts, they have a strong belief in the powers of, and reverence for, those expert in making rain.

For many tribes right across northern Australia, these powers rest with the Kendi, the cruel frilled dragons whose totems are the wild elements of thunder, lightning, wind, hail and rain. These frilled dragons created the great flood that drowned most things then living in the Dreamtime.

There was a time when the animals, birds and reptiles bred so rapidly that the land could no longer support them. Fighting for food and shelter was a daily occurrence.

So the tribes assembled to discuss their plight. It was suggested that the birds might seek out another land to live in since they were best equipped to travel, but they refused. Some other suggestions were made but, after many days, nothing had been agreed.

Tiring of the fruitless discussions, the Kendi decided on their own solution. Climbing to the tops of the surrounding mountains, they painted themselves with fat and red ochre and bands of white pipeclay. Then, cutting themselves with stone knives until blood flowed down their bodies, they began their chant to call up the greatest storm.

It came with deafening thunder, blinding spears of lightning, winds that uprooted the largest trees and rain that did not stop until the land was flooded and only the highest hilltops remained above the water.

In this great flood, most living things drowned - a horrible demonstration of the will of the Kendi who remain today the most powerful of the rainmakers.

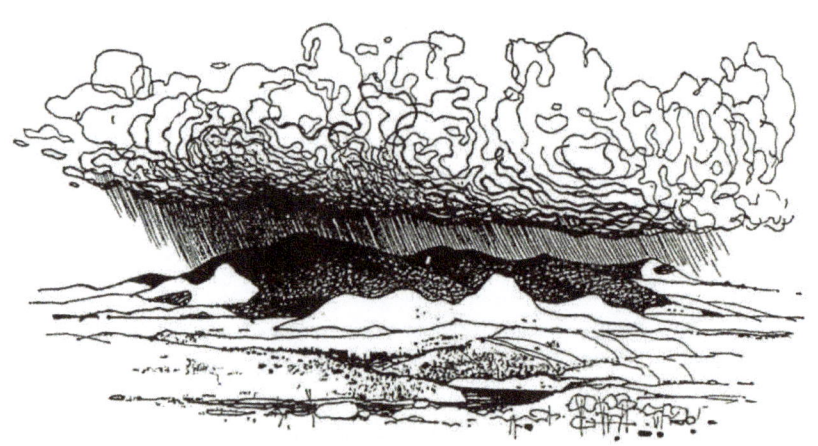

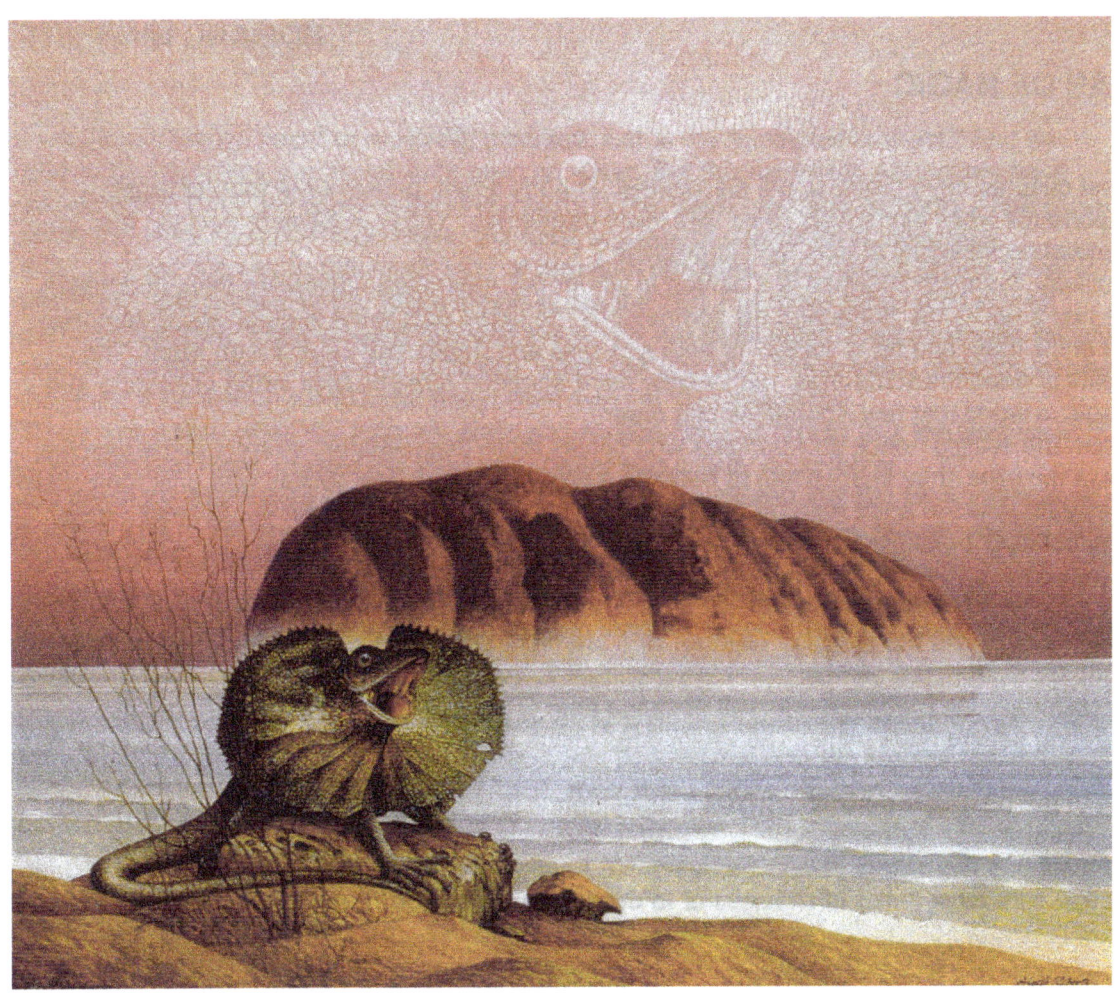

Mr and Mrs Charles E Hulley

THE RAINMAKERS

The strong faith in the awesome power of the rainmakers is common to many Aboriginal tribes, particularly those who occupy the dry areas north and south of Alice Springs, tribes such as the Arunta, Kaitish and Unmatjira peoples.

Among their many Dream time ancestors were Irria, Inungamella and Ilpailurkna who were potent rainmakers, men whose magical gifts could make the barren deserts bloom.

Irria's rain-making rituals centred around the black cockatoo, the bird appointed by the Dreamtime spirits to bring thunder and lightning down from the north. Only Irria could wear cockatoo feathers in his hair.

Irria taught Inungamella how to make rain and gave him many gypsum stones which, when correctly sung over, produced the rain clouds which they resembled.

Upailurkna's magical power was associated with the yam stick. This was painted with red ochre and decorated with white feathers which, when blown off into the sky, were transformed into clouds.

And where these ancestors established totem rain-centres, their namesakes used the same magic to conjure up rain well into the present century. Even today these areas are lush and green and have a relatively high rainfall.

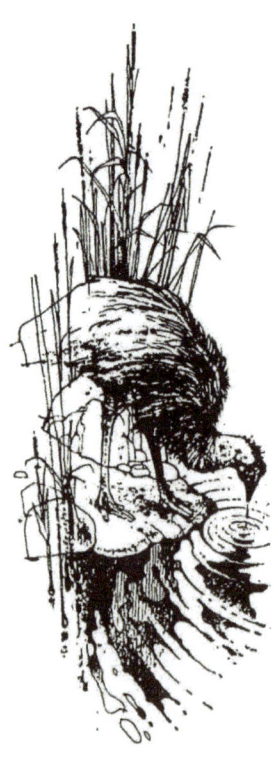

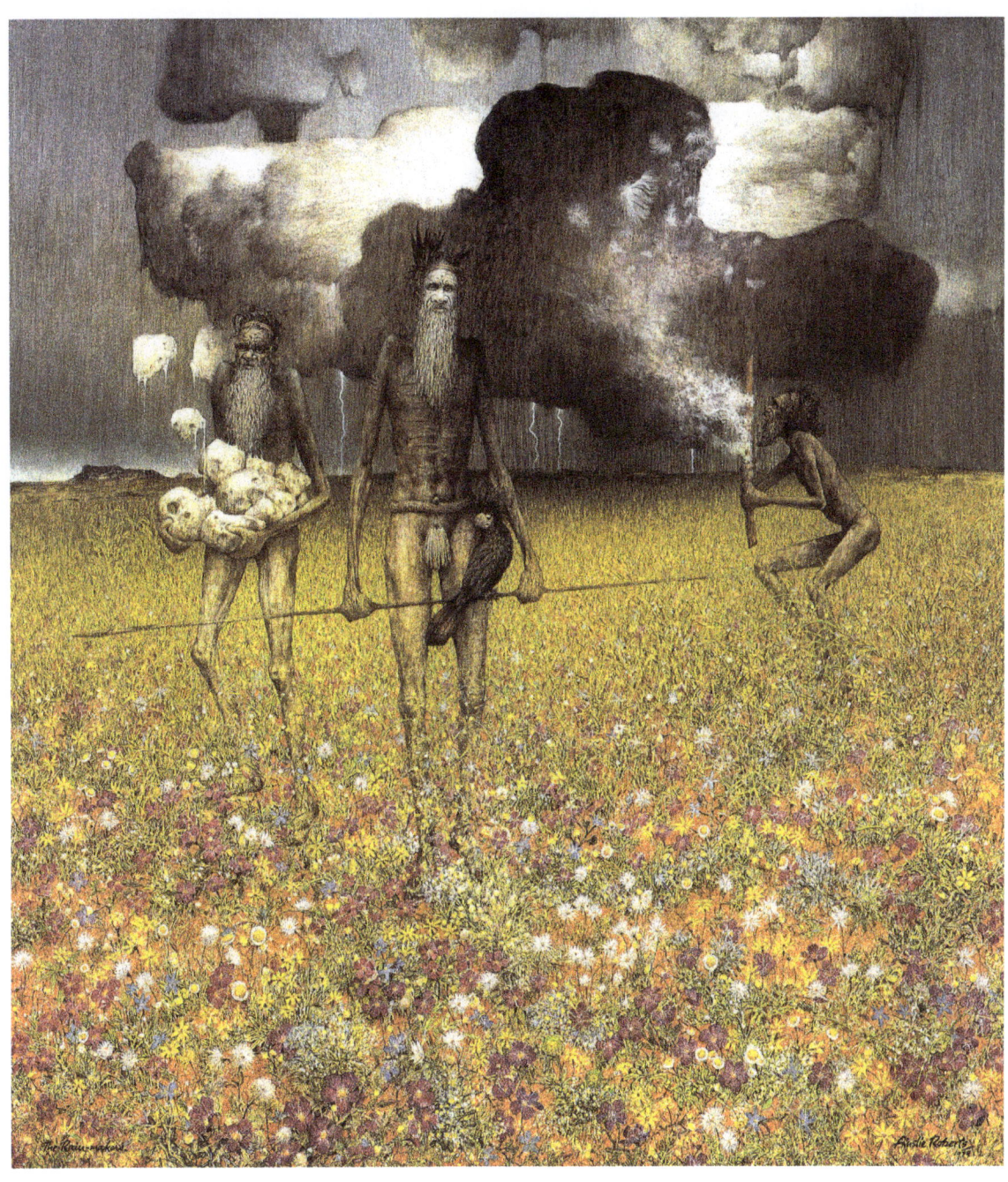

Mr Samuel and Mrs Wendy Olenik

DARAMBAL OF THE DREAMTIME

Australia abounds in wonderful flora. Many magnificent species are unique to this country.

Flowers are not only beautiful themselves but have represented the harmony of the world since man first scratched his feelings on a cave wall. Joy, love, peace, national pride, rapture - all are expressed in floral images. The waterlily is one of nature's most exquisite flowers. Throughout history it has been regarded as a symbol of fertility.

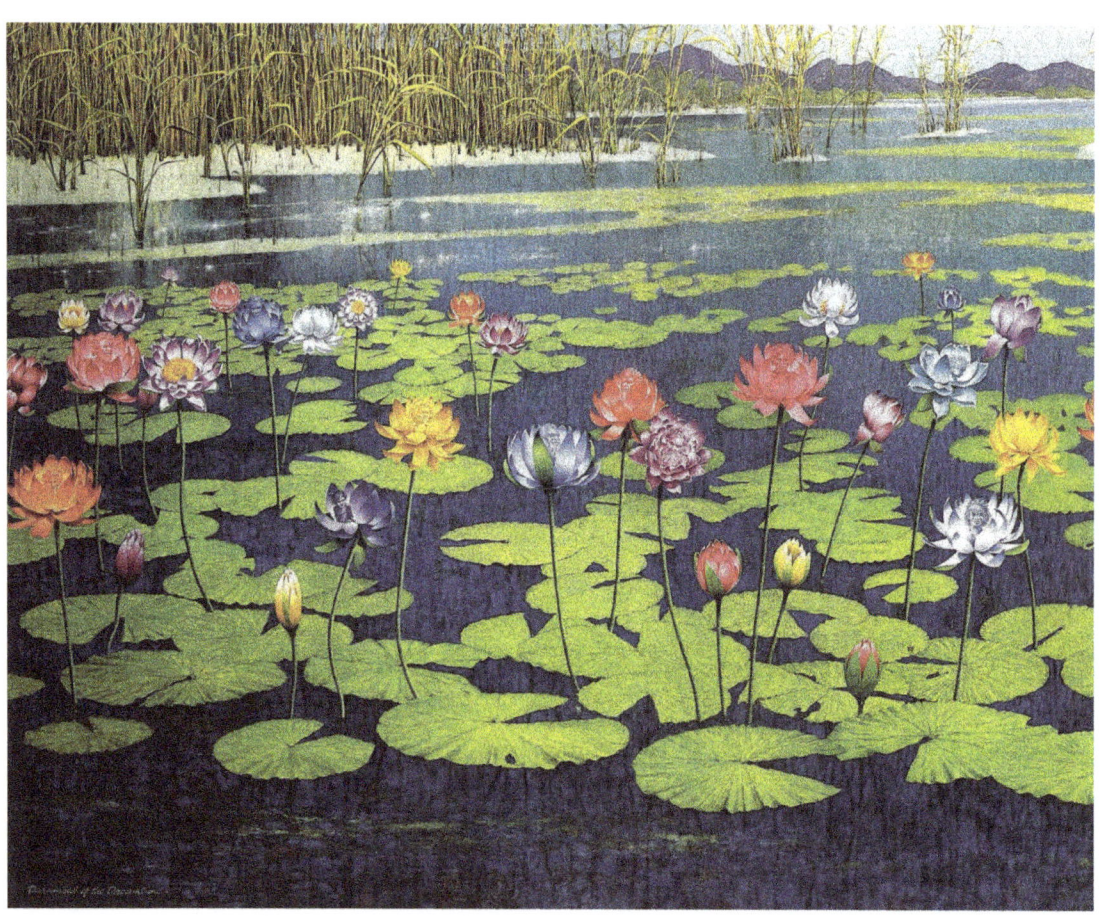

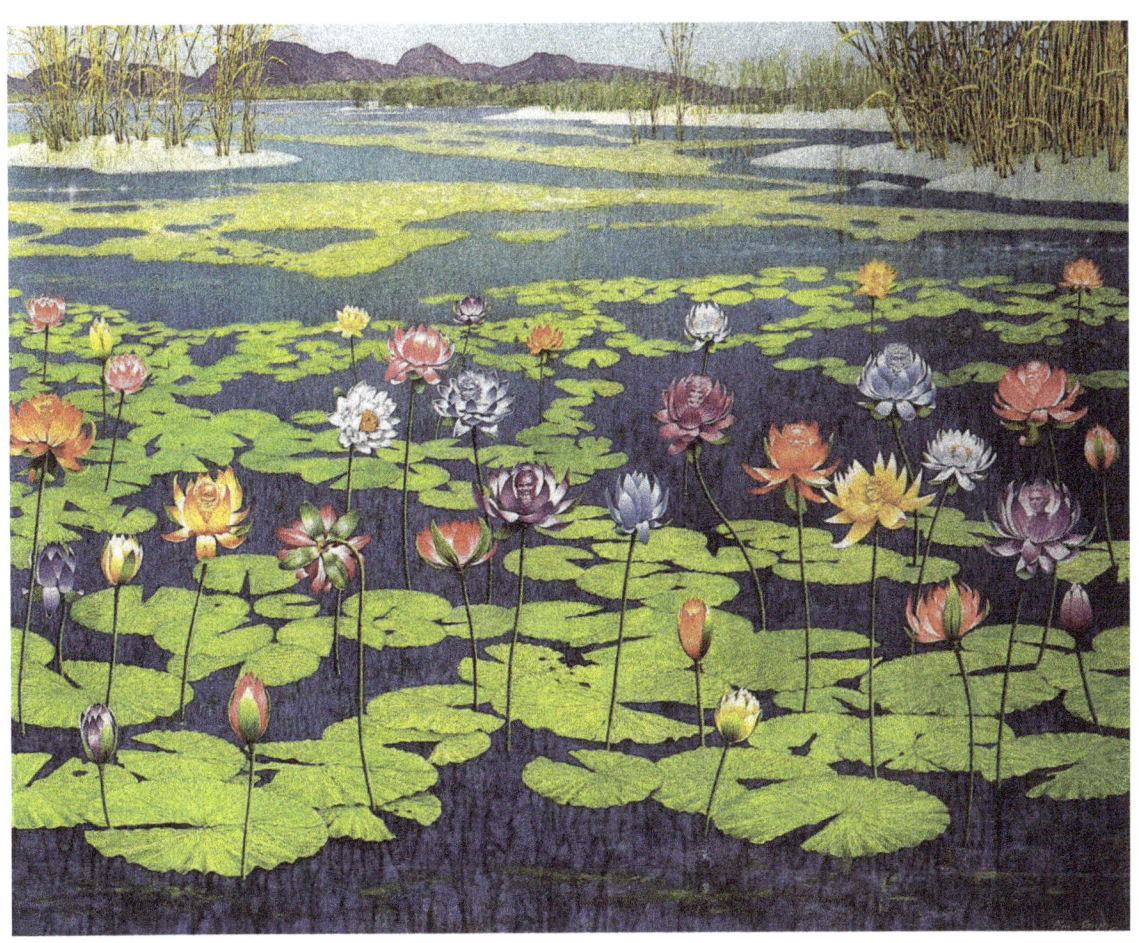

The Aboriginal word 'Darambal' means waterlily and the waterlily flower is the totemic Dreamtime ancestor of the Darambal tribe. This tribe lived in the Rockhampton area for more than 40,000 years, occupying the coastal portion of the Fitzroy Region from Shoalwater Bay in the north to the mouth of the Fitzroy River in the south. The Fitzroy Region is one of Queensland's major river systems. Its waters converge to form the Fitzroy River and the many lagoons around the Rockhampton area, lagoons in which waterlilies grow in profusion. This painting is a symbolic interpretation of the Dreamtime origin of the Darambal tribe of Aborigines. It hangs in the Dreamtime Cultural Centre.

BANISHMENT OF THE GOANNA

Our daily news reports are constantly full of man's inhumanity to man. And how often is greed the motivation?

But the Australian Aborigines have always lived by a strict moral code. Selfishness is not tolerated; meanness is punished.

Many of their myths are moral parables which explain their rules of behaviour. One such myth relates how the selfish Goanna-men were outwitted by their wives, the Gecko-women.

During a great drought, the Goanna-men had a secret waterhole which they would share with no-one but their own tribe. But their wives, seeing so many others, young and old, dying of thirst, decided to find the waterhole so that everyone could share it.

They told their men that one of the women (who was actually hiding in the hills) had been kidnapped. The Goanna-men immediately suspected the men of the neighbouring Emu tribe and set off to fight them.

Once the men were out of the way, the women began their search. When they found the spring that fed the waterhole, the women drove a magical stick deep into the opening in the hillside. Immediately the water poured out in a torrent to form a huge river, and all the people from the other tribes were at last able to drink.

The evil Goanna-men were furious. They had lost not only their secret waterhole but their power to hurt others. The Gecko-women climbed to the top of a large gum tree where, to escape their husbands' anger, they changed themselves into the little gecko lizards that live under the bark of trees today.

For their sins, the spirits banished the men from the area and sent them to live forever as goannas in the great red sandhills and the dry open plains.

This story was often told to Aboriginal children to teach them that water belongs to everybody and that those who disobey this law must be punished.

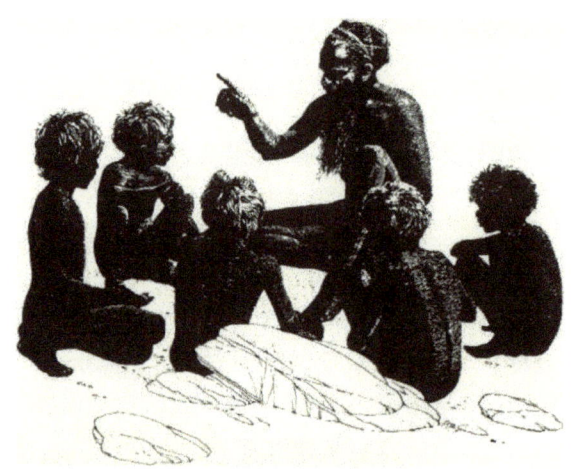

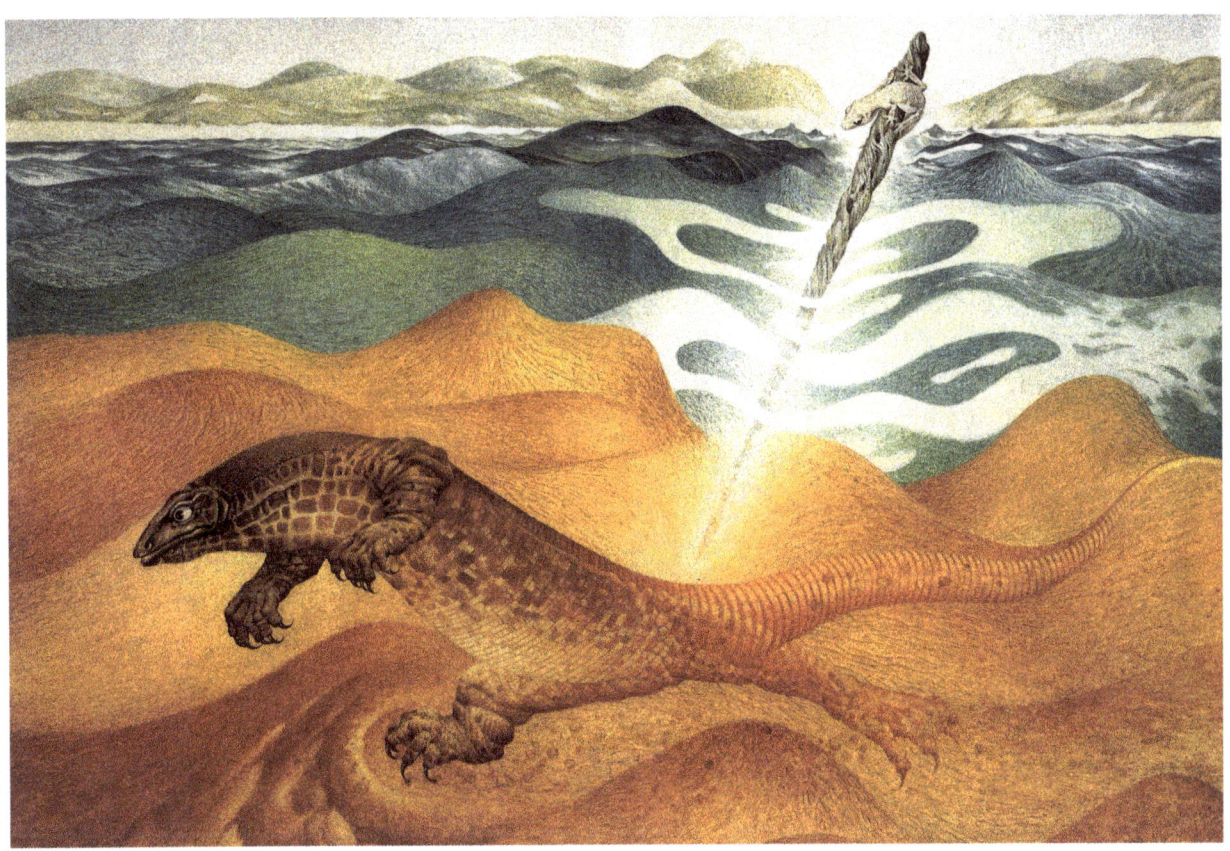

Private Collection

YULU'S CHARCOAL

The world's dwindling fuel supply is a constant source of concern to the nations who consume it and the nations who provide it. In Australia, we are 'reliably informed' that the majority of our deposits of coal will be depleted by the end of this century.

The huge coal fields of Leigh Creek in South Australia were first discovered by white men in 1888 when coal-bearing shale was found during the construction of a railway dam. But the old Aborigines of the Flinders Ranges area insisted that they knew about the coal deposits long before the coming of the white man. They called them Yulu's Charcoal, and Dreamtime mythology explains the origin of these deposits.

Yulu Yulura was a giant Aboriginal ancestor who decided to attend an initiation ceremony to be held in the place we know today as Wilpena Pound. During his long journey eastwards to the Pound, Yulu lit many fires to announce his coming.

These fires were so extensive and used up so many trees that the charcoal left behind formed the present coal deposits and caused the vast treeless areas to the west of the Flinders Ranges.

The first open cut mining in the 1940s disclosed that one of the coal basins was indeed burnt out, and the later discovery of the burnt shales of the Northern Basin was further confirmation of Yulu's spectacular journey of so long ago.

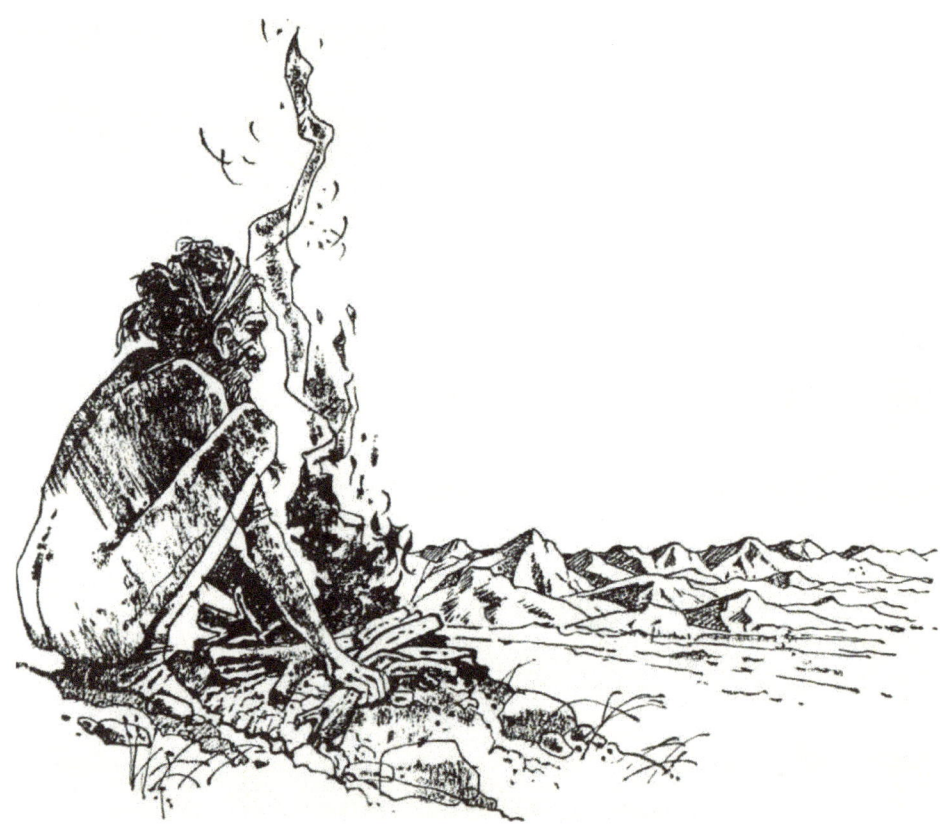

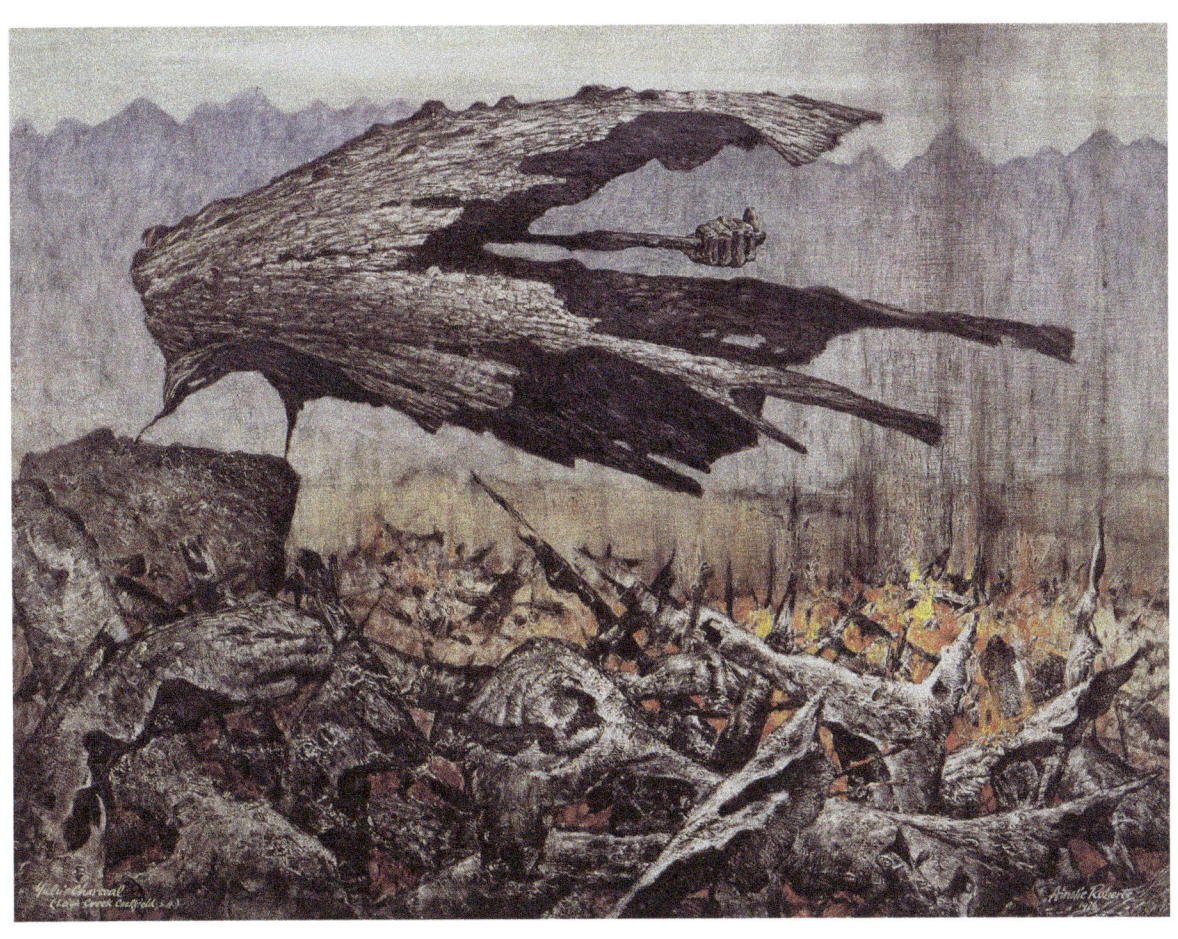

Mr and Mrs Charles E Hulley

THE EAGLE AND THE DINGO

Sadly, Australia's native dog, the dingo, has developed something of a notorious reputation. This is no surprise to either farmers or the Aborigines who have always known of that beast's evil nature.

For long ago, the Aborigines who lived on Melville Island, north of Darwin, collected their best ochres from Arunumpi on the island's southern shores. At this place there are two large ochre deposits, one of yellow and another of white, which were used in their ceremonies for body decoration and for painting their unique burial poles.

But the locality has another special significance. The tribal mythology relates how, during the great creation period, Mudati and his wife Kirijuna were camped at this spot when Mudati saw his wife's brother, Jurumu, coming towards them.

Mudati warned his wife not to speak nor even look at her brother, for so it had been decreed by the spirits. But the woman, who had not seen her brother since they were children, took a quick look to see how much he had grown.

Instantly, she dropped dead at her husband's feet. He saw her body slowly transform into the first dingo and rise to its feet and slink away. The brother, Jurumu, was changed into the eagle.

Ever since then, the dingo, ashamed of its disobedient action in those far-off times, keeps out of sight and has developed an uncanny ability to merge with its surroundings.

The dingo slinking through the bush and the eagle soaring high above it, remind Aborigines of Melville Island of the ancient spirit law: that once brothers and sisters have grown to be adults, they may no longer look at or speak to each other.

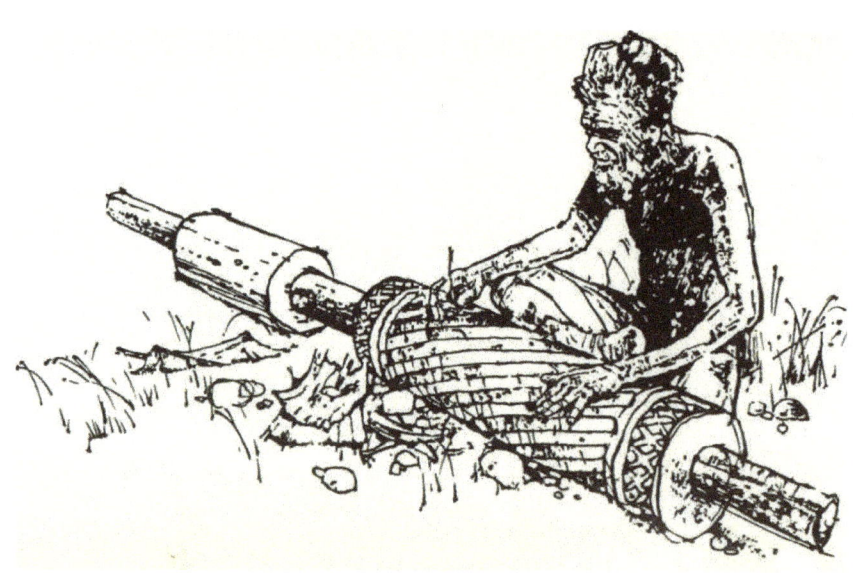

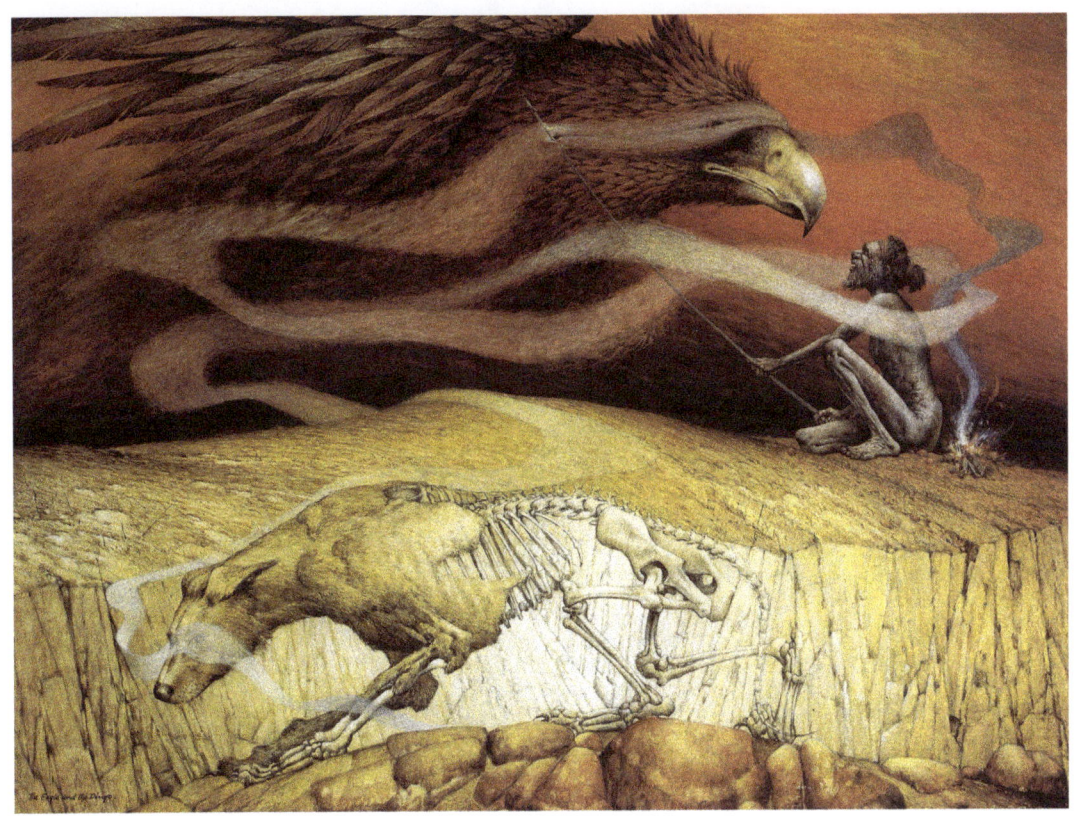

Private Collection

THE BONEFISH TREE

The Aborigines of the coastal and river regions of Australia are traditionally excellent fishermen. They know where the best fish are biting, when the tides are right and how to catch the biggest fish when others can net only tiddlers. Their Compleat Angler was written in the Dreamtime.

This myth from northern Australia relates how the hunters of the tribe are able to increase the supply of bonefish (bony bream) which, like all food that is taken from the rivers and the sea, varies in quantity from one season to another.

In the beginning, when all the creatures, birds and plants of Australia had human form, Wilkalla the bonefish-man quarrelled violently with his sister. During the fight, he threw a spear at her. It sank so deeply into her head that she could not draw it out again so she transformed herself into the mangrove. Today, Wilkalla's spear is the stalk which rises from the mud when a new mangrove plant is growing. Ever since then, the mangrove seeds have been an important item in the diet of the Aborigines.

But before Wilkalla's sister transformed herself into the mangrove, she struck Wilkalla a fatal blow across the back with her digging stick. As he was dying, he called to the other hunters of his tribe to carry him to a huge bloodwood tree standing on the banks of the river.

His spirit went deep into the roots of the tree which draw water from the river. It stayed there forever to make sure that the tribe would always have enough fish for their food supply.

To this day, whenever the fishing is poor, the tribe knows that if they hit the bloodwood trees along the river, Wilkalla's spirit will send many fish out into the water for them to catch. And the bonefish still carries on his back the mark of his sister's digging stick.

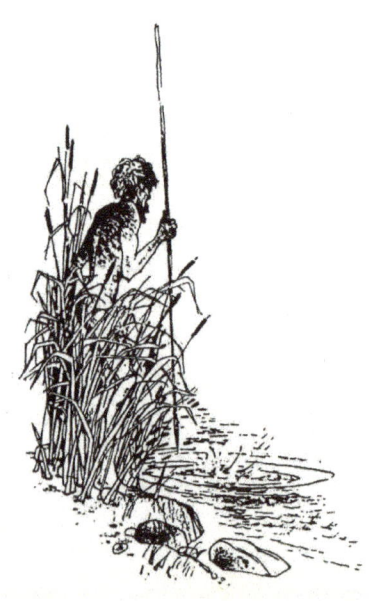

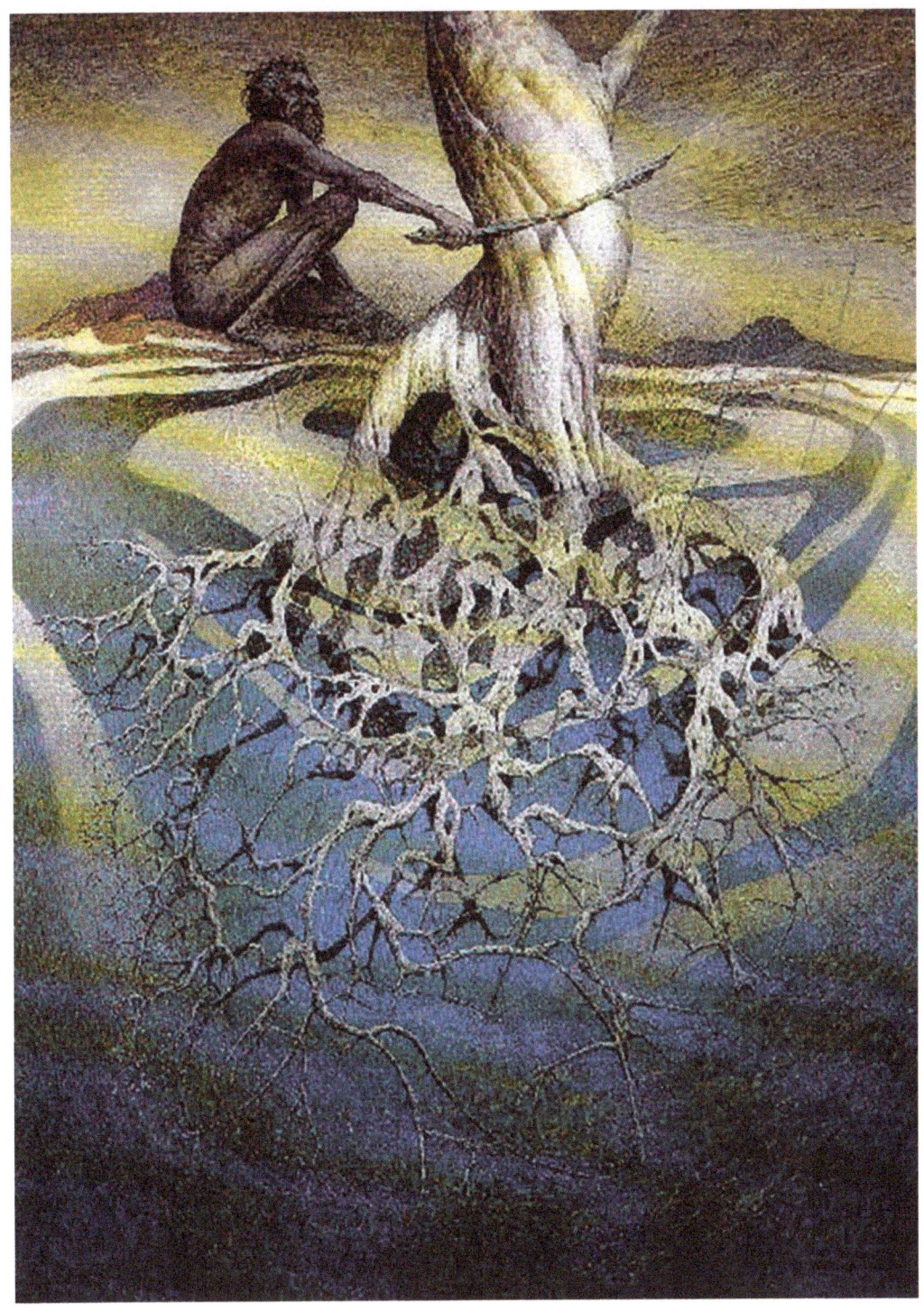

Private Collection

ABDUCTION OF THE WHITE SWANS

Another Aboriginal myth with an 'enemies and allies' theme is the story of how Australian swans became black.

For in the Dreamtime, there were no black swans. All of them were white. This remained so until the time came when two swans landed on a lagoon on Australia's north coast, not knowing that the lagoon was the property of the eagles. The eagles, angry with this trespass, savagely attacked the two swans and tore out most of their feathers. The eagles then picked up the swans and carried them far to the south where they left them in the great desert to die, bald and unprotected.

But as they lay in agony, the swans heard the call of the black crows. Looking up, they saw a huge flock of them above. As they flew over, each of the crows plucked a black feather from its own body and let it fall on the swans.

"The eagles are our enemies, too", they called. "Our feathers will clothe you and help you grow strong again."

And so the swans recovered and flew on south where today the black feathers of the crows cover almost every part of the swans' bodies. But the white feathers on their wing tips and the blood on their beaks are reminders that the eagles are still their enemies.

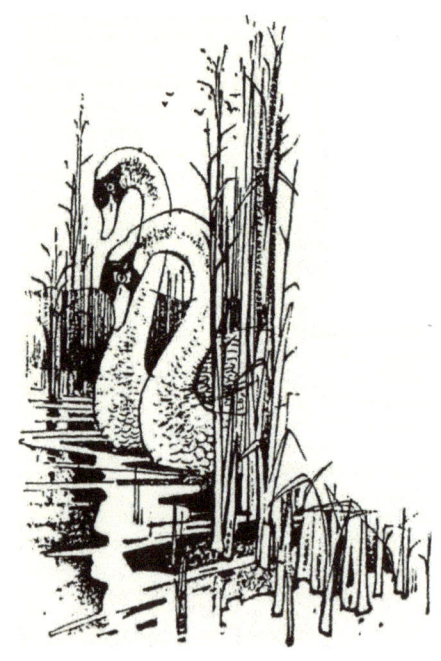

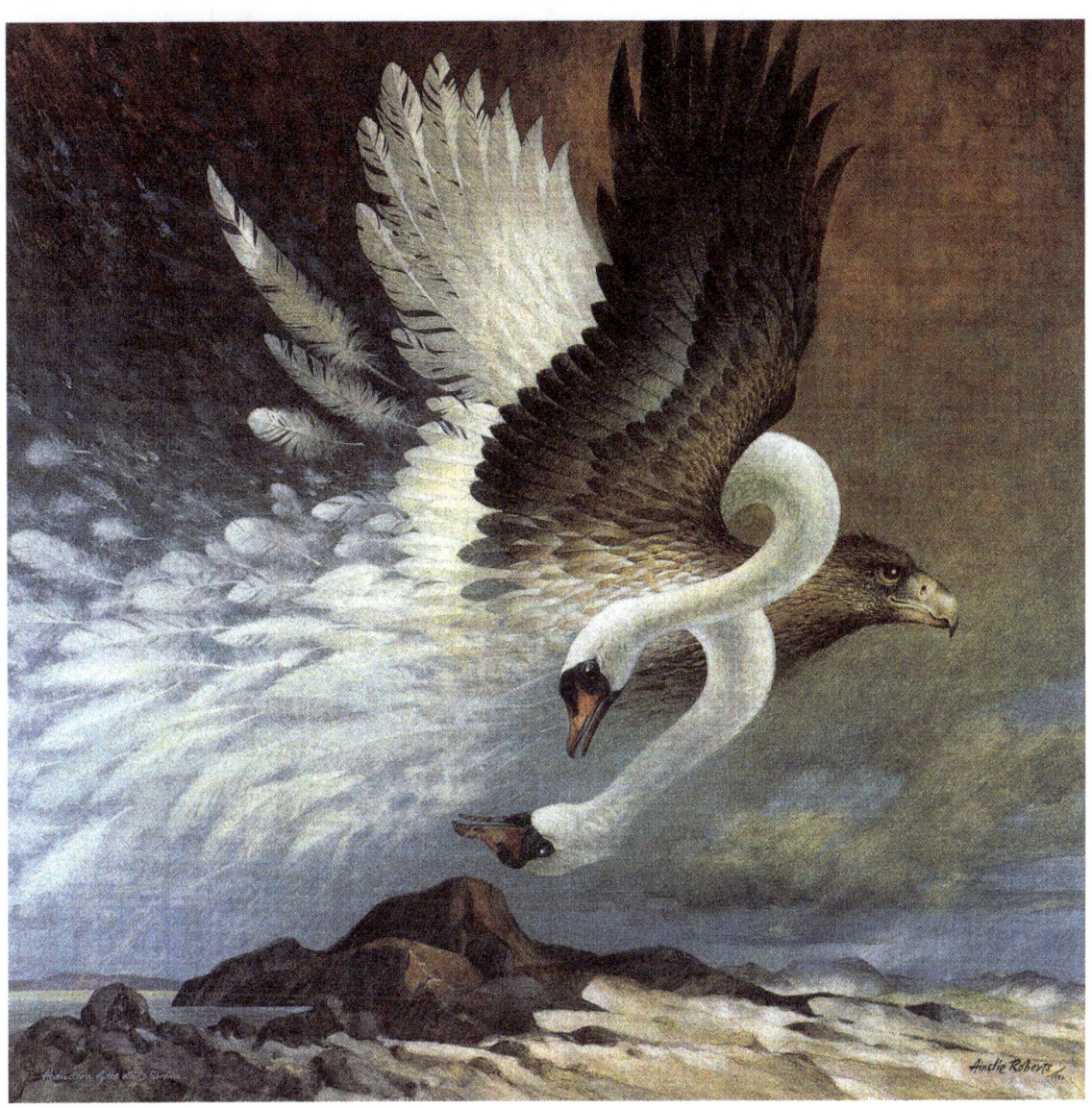

Miss Allyson Parsons

JIRAKUPAI AND HERONS

Man is a territorial creature, fiercely protective of that portion of the world he believes is his. Today we erect fences around our homes to repel unwanted or uninvited visitors to our small plot. In times past, the castle walls were fortressed.

Throughout history, nationalism has expanded individual territorial claims. Countries have fought - and are still fighting - to protect or reclaim 'their' land from invasion.

Aboriginal tribes, too, have strict boundaries to their land. During earliest times, each tribal area was reserved. No member was permitted to venture beyond it and no outsiders were allowed to enter.

But once a party of Melville Island men on walkabout ignored these tribal boundaries and wandered into forbidden territory. There they saw Jirakupai and his two wives beside a lagoon.

Jirakupai was famed as an expert in making barbed spears. He had just finished making a number of these weapons when the enemy Melville Island men rushed into his camp and, jealous of his skill, speared him in his back many times. But as they struck, Jirakupai plucked the spears out and cast them back at his attackers. Then, howling loudly with pain, he picked up the spears he had just made and dived into the water to escape further injury. His wives, to avoid capture, changed themselves into birds and can be seen today as the herons that frequent the many mangrove swamps.

The next morning, his enemies saw Jirakupai floating in the water - no longer as a man but as a crocodile. The spear wounds in his back had grown into a spinal crest; his mouth, through shouting so much in his pain, had grown longer and larger; and his bundle of spears had been transformed into the vicious barbed tail.

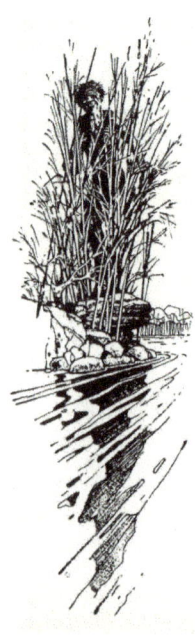

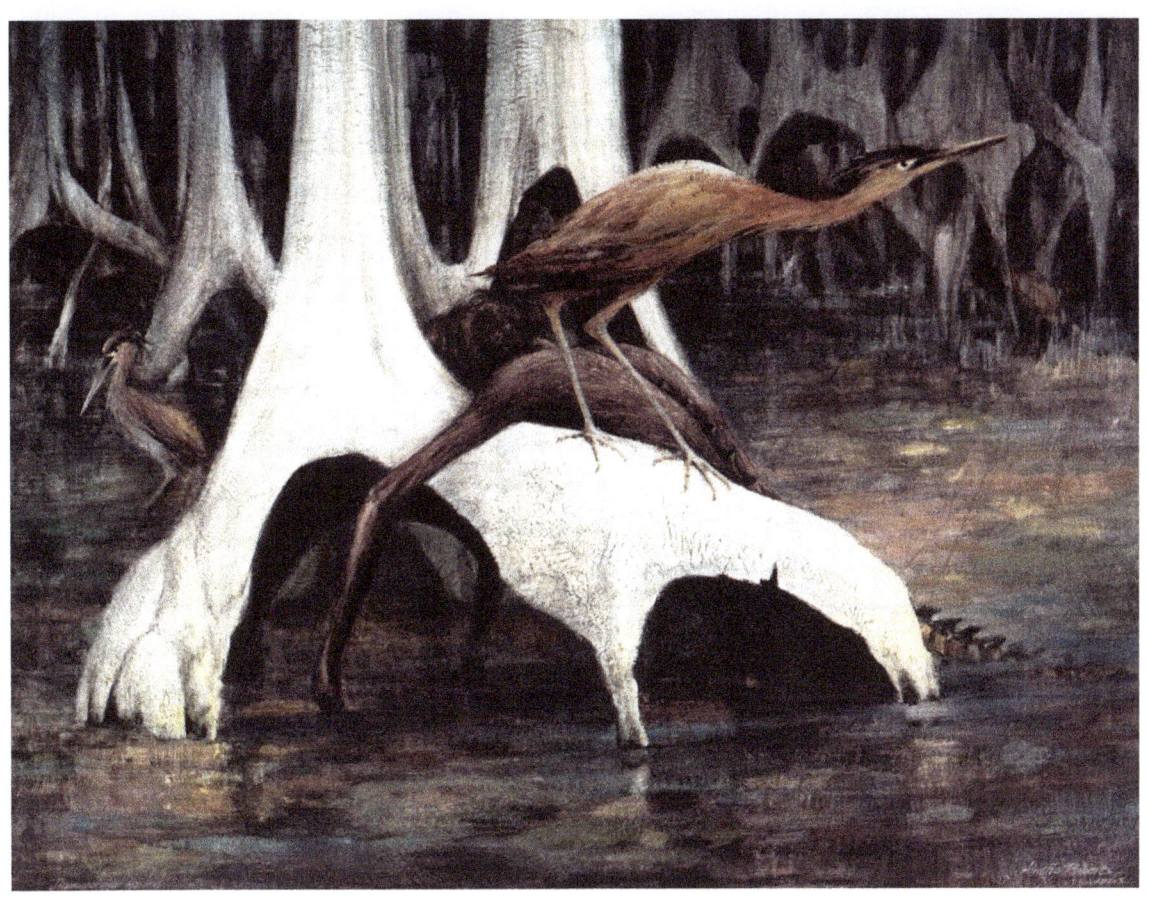

Mr Burke M Hyde Jnr

THE FIRST DEATH

For every beginning there is an end. The growing plant that began from a seed may be soon cut down. The butterfly that crawls from its crysalid flutters its wings for only a few weeks. A child is born and his death is inevitable.

For many cultures, death is only a beginning. Beliefs in resurrection, reincarnation and an afterlife are universal.

In the Dream time days of the Australian Aborigines, there was no finality to life. But this, too, came to an end.

Purukupali, one of the great creators of the Tiwi tribe of Melville Island, had an infant son, Jinini, whom he loved very much. But one day Jinini's mother, Bima, neglected him while she was with her lover, Japara, and Jinini died. When he heard of the child's death, Purukupali became so enraged that he beat his wife over the head with a throwing-stick and hunted her into the jungle. He then attacked her lover with a club and covered his face with deep wounds.

Despite this, Japara wanted to help the anguished father restore his son to life. But Purukupali angrily refused the offer. He picked up the dead body of his son and walked into the sea, calling loudly as the waters closed over his head, "As I die, so all must die and never again come to life!" - a decree that brought death to all the world.

The place where Purukupali drowned himself is nowa large and dangerous whirlpool in Dundas Strait between Melville Island and the mainland. Here the current is so swift and strong that any Aborigine attempting to cross the maelstrom in a canoe risks being drowned.

When Japara saw what had happened, he changed himself into the moon and rose into the sky, his face still bearing the scars of his wounds. But although Japara cannot entirely escape the decree of Purukupali and has to die for three days each month, he is eternally reincarnated. Bima, mother of the dead Jinini, was changed into a curlew who even now roams the forest at night, wailing with sorrow over the loss of her son and the calamity she brought to the world.

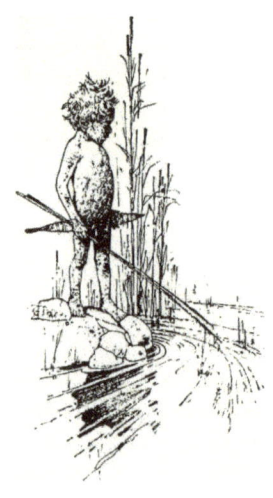

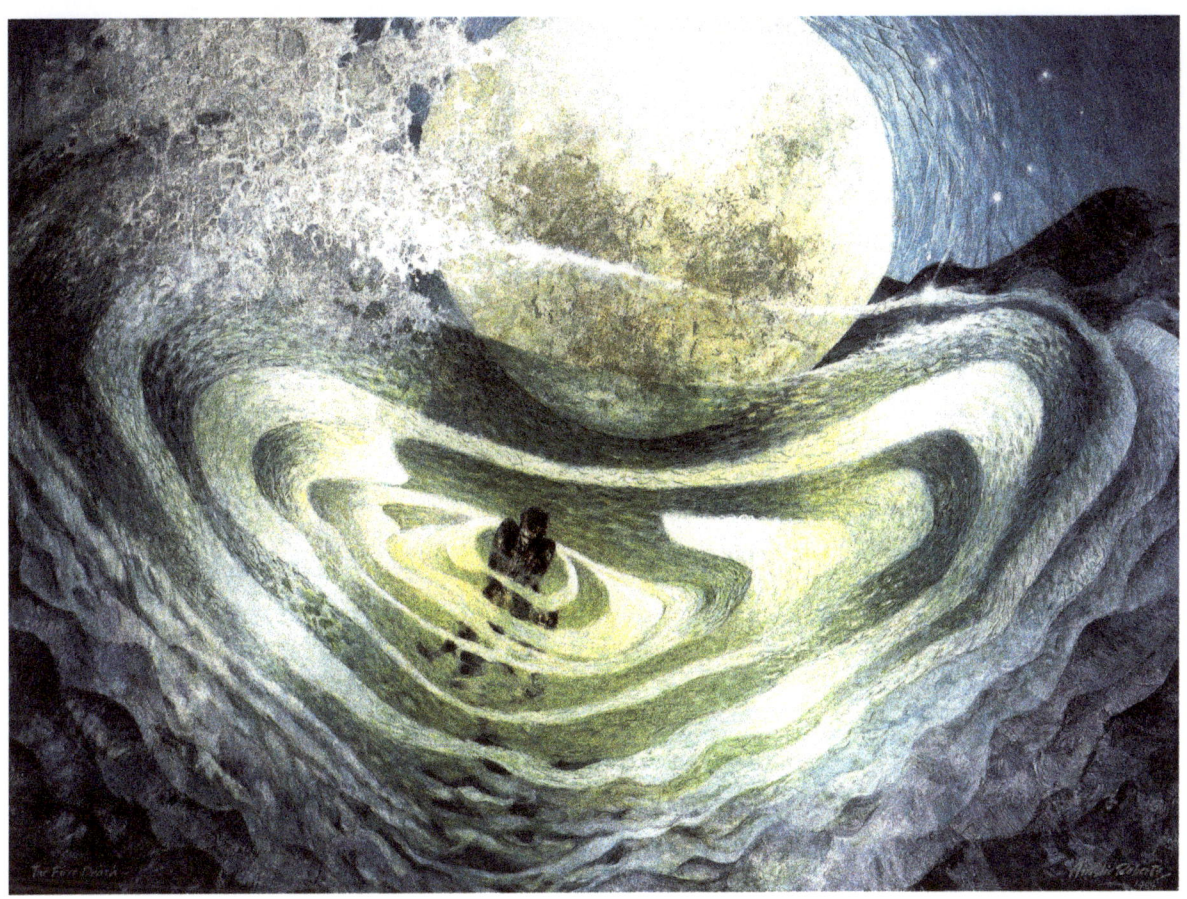

Private Collection

MOPADITI

Dying, and whatever you believe happens after death, is as much a part of living as being born.

To the Tiwi people of Melville Island, life after death plays a significant role in their daily activities. For their ancestors believed that the spirits of the dead, the Mopaditis, lived in self-contained communities. They resembled Aborigines in appearance but their bodies were only wraiths of their former beings.

The Pukamuni burial ceremonies were designed to speed these spirits to their future home. When the ceremony was complete, the spirit set out on its long flight, escorted by black cockatoos who warned the inhabitants of the Aboriginal 'heaven' that a new Mopaditi was on its way.

Once safely lodged in its eternal home, a Mopaditi normally remained there. But a lonely Mopaditi who awaited the conclusion of the Pukamuni ceremony, or one who had lost its way, was believed to be a great danger to the living. The Aborigines believed that a lonely Mopaditi would steal the spirit of some living person to keep it company and took every precaution not to be seen or recognised by one of them.

An Aborigine could always sense when a Mopaditi was following closely after him, intent on stealing his spirit. To protect himself, the victim would carry a torch of flaming bark, shout loudly as he walked through the bush or attempt to disguise himself in some way. But if all these precautions failed, he would die, and even the magic of the medicine-men was unlikely to save him.

Now and again, a party of Mopaditis who had recently arrived in their new home would return to a camping place they used on earth to watch the burial rites of an old friend. When the ceremonies were over and the living were asleep, the spirit people would repeat the same rituals until the glow of the sun-woman in the eastern sky warned them that they must hasten back to their new home.

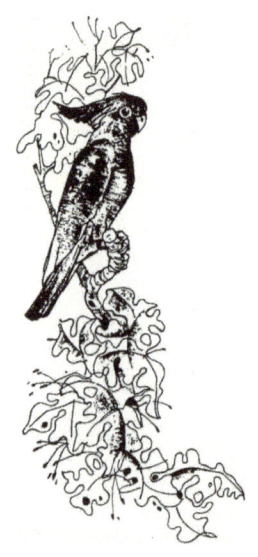

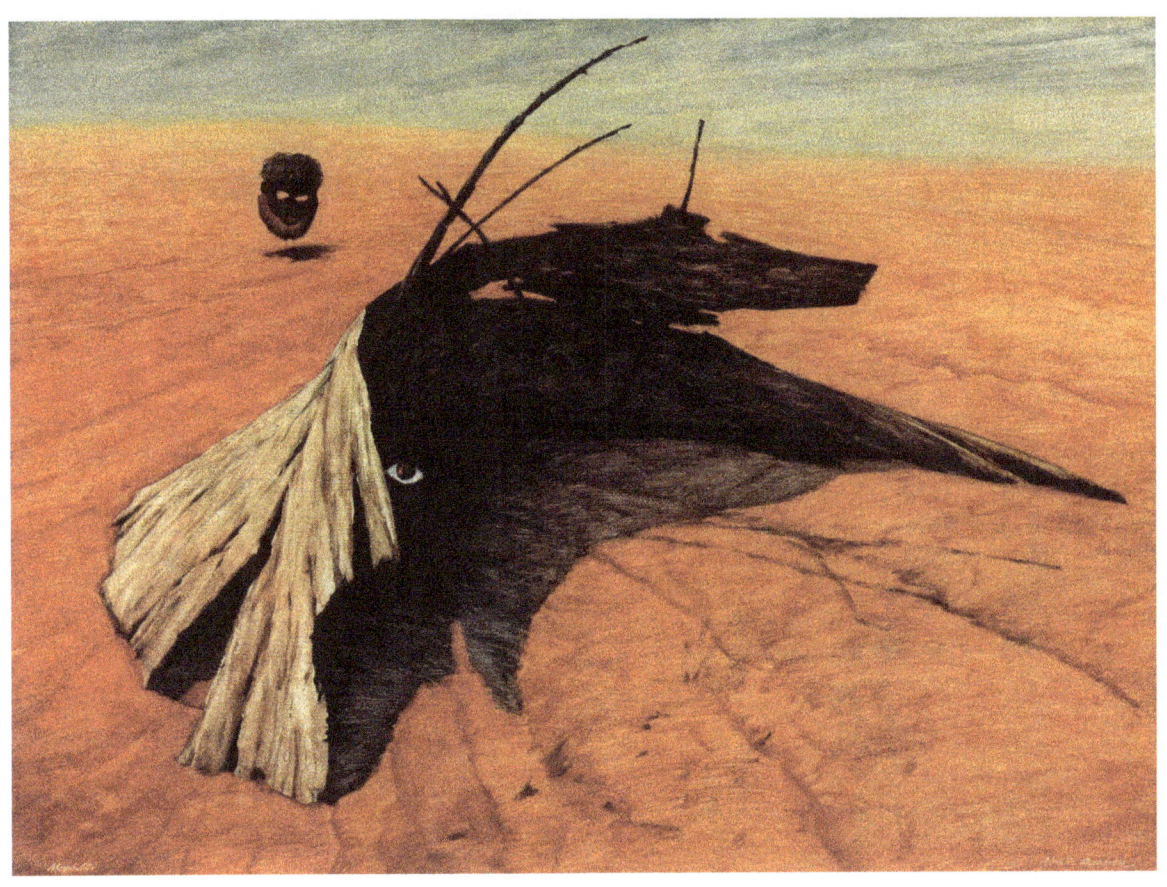

Mr Burke M Hyde Jnr

THE GYMEA

One hot clay in the long-ago Dreamtime, an Aboriginal tribe took refuge from a violent summer storm in one of the many huge caves in the mountains of New South Wales. The great deluge of rain caused a landslide which blocked the narrow entrance to the cave.

The imprisoned tribe, terrified and in darkness, seemed to be doomed. But Bullana, the strongest and most courageous of the tribal warriors, found a narrow crevice which led up to the surface. He pulled and squeezed himself up until he emerged into the sunlight. But none of the others was strong enough to follow him.

Bullana was determined to do all in his power to keep his people alive. Day after day he hunted and speared fish in the river. He made a long rope to lower food down into the cave. Many times each day he climbed up the mountain to let food down to his tribe which now depended on him.

At last this constant heavy work and responsibility had its effect upon even Bullana's strength. One day he slipped and fell into a ravine, breaking so many bones that he was almost unable to go on. But although he was exhausted and in so much pain that he could only crawl, he still tried to hunt and fish for his tribe.

The effort was hopeless, and those in the cave began to die. Finally, Bullana knew he must abandon his struggle to save them and he collapsed among the tangled undergrowth of his beloved valley.

As he died, his hand grasped a small plant. And as the spirit left his body, this plant instantly grew into a mass of long broad leaves and the great white flowers which burst from the centre became red with his blood. This is the plant which we know today as the gymea or gigantic lily, and it gains its strength from the spirit of Bullana.

Countless centuries after the sudden growth of the gymea, a group of white men discovered a way into the huge old cave and found that the floor was covered with the tangled skeletons of Bullana's tribe.

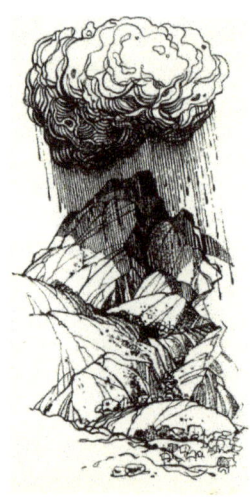

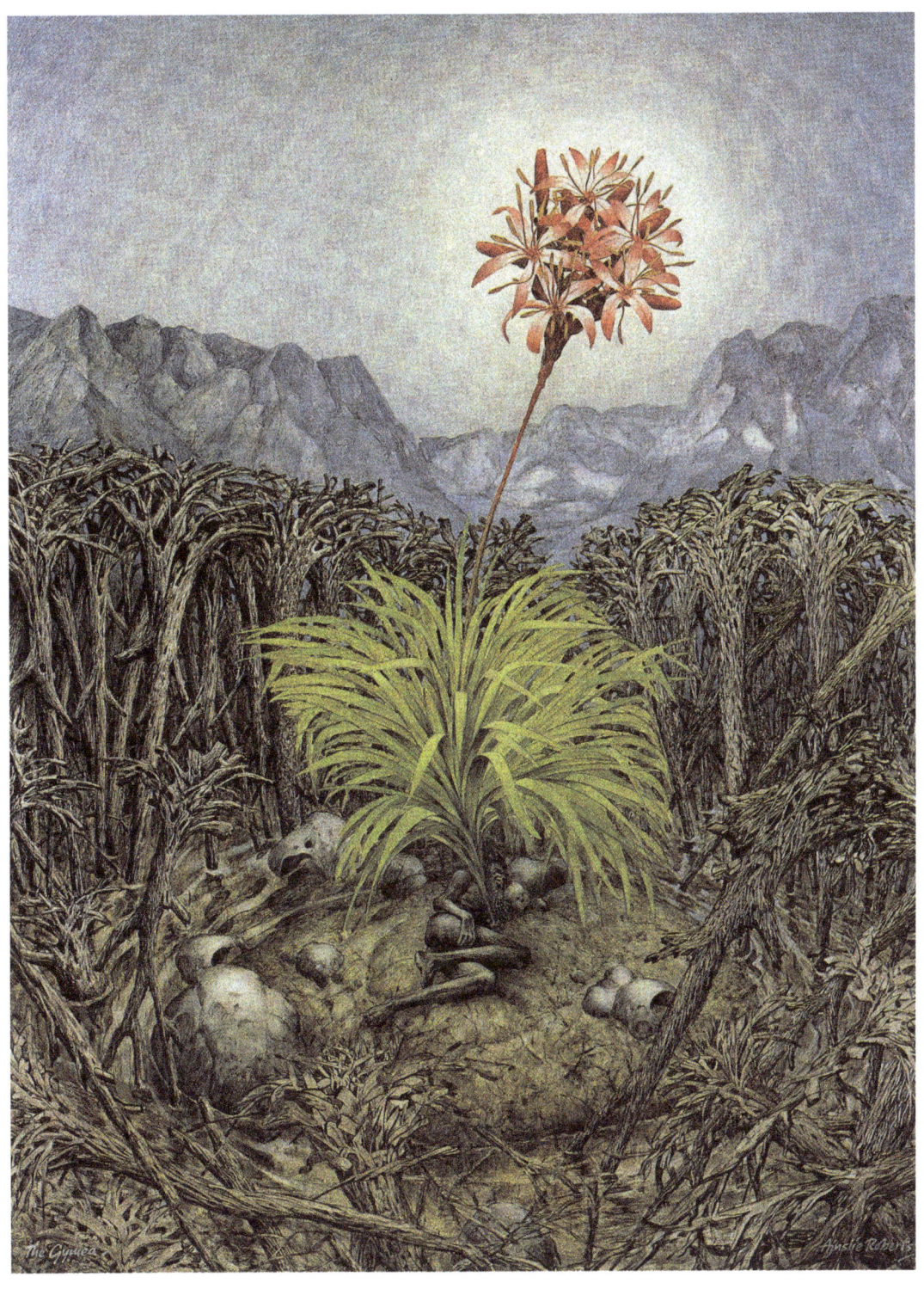

Commander and Mrs R Brasch

MAN OF MAGIC

Most cultures have professional hierarchies. In early times, priests were men of great importance while alchemists rated with lowly tradesmen. Today in western society, the medical professional stands high in prestige.

Similarly, the medicine-man is a person in whom the Australian Aborigines have much faith. He has a family, he hunts with his companions, he takes part in the secular and ceremonial life of his tribe and he is subject to both sickness and death. But he is a man apart. The spirits of dead medicine-men, the Wulgis, have admitted him into their world of healing and magic, a world that few Aborigines can enter.

When the Wulgis notice an Aborigine who shows more than ordinary interest in the psychic life of the tribe, they choose him to become a medicine-man. The Wulgis wait until the initiate is asleep, take the spirit from his body and change it into the form of an eagle-hawk. Then they conduct it into the sky where it is shown the secrets of magic and healing which are known only to the medicine-men.

On return to his ordinary life, the newly initiated medicine-man has many new powers: he can heal the sick, find the spirits of children who are lost in the darkness and hunt the malignant night-spirits from the camps.

Occasionally the medicine-man will seek the help of a Wulgi spirit to cure an Aboriginal suffering severe body pains. The Wulgi goes inside the patient and searches until it finds an object such as a stick or stone which has been placed there by an enemy. The Wulgi gives this to the medicine-man who shows it as evidence that the cause of the pain has been removed.

It is said that the patient always recovers. No Aborigine ever doubts the ability of a medicine-man to cure most forms of sickness or to overcome the effects of evil spirits.

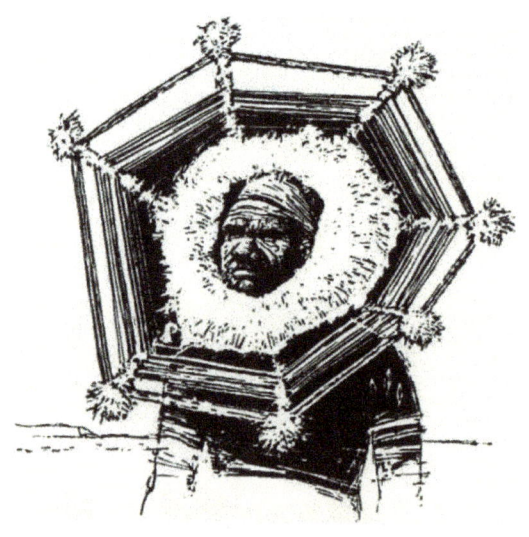

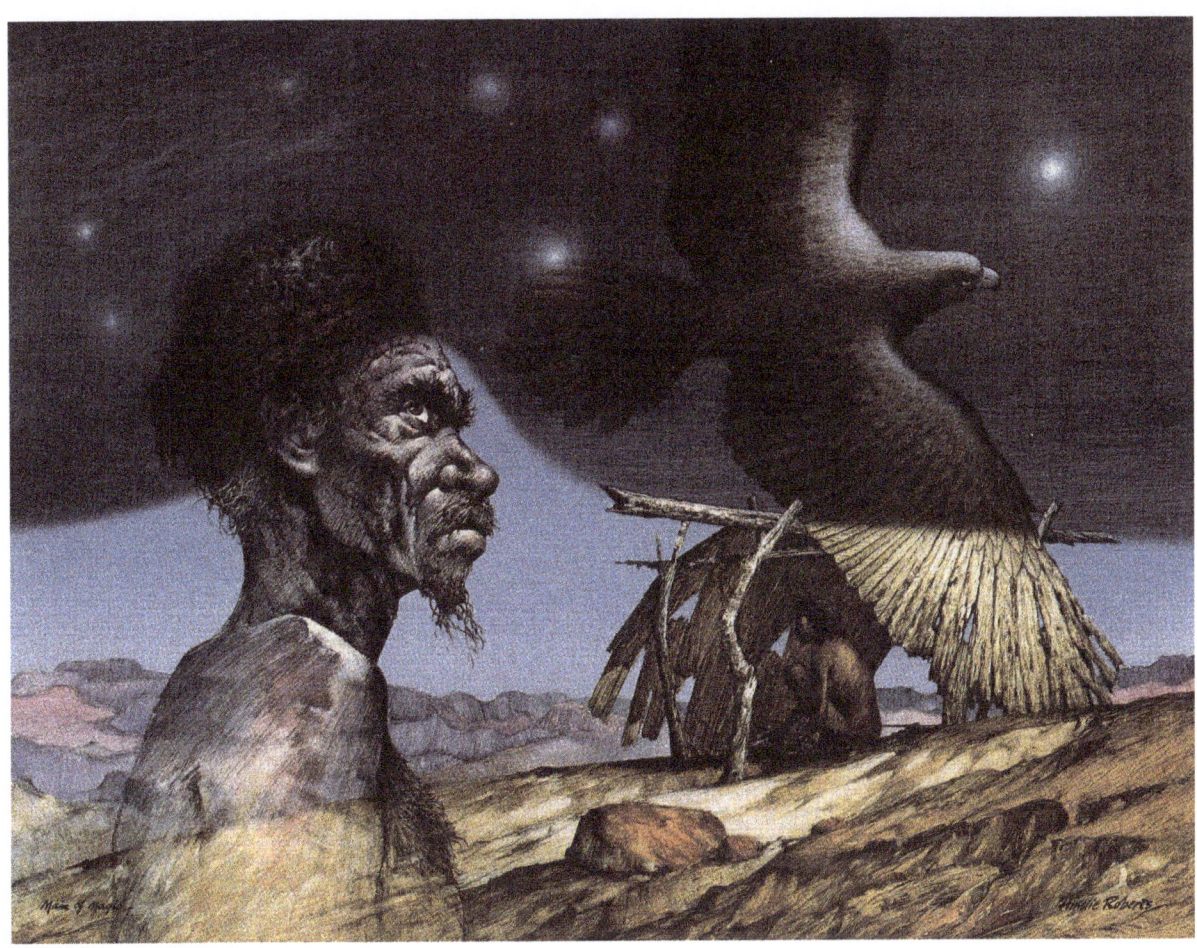

Private Collection

THE LAST HURRICANE

In our ecologically conscious society, we hear often of the dangers to our world of upsetting the 'balance of nature'. For nature had it all organised before egotistical man thought he could do it better.

One of nature's most basic laws is that all creatures have a purpose. To the cynic, the purpose may be just his monetary or gastronomical gain. To the Aborigines, birds, fish, mammals, insects and reptiles all have a specific function.

Indeed, they have great respect for the birds of the air. Many of them play an important role in the daily lives of the tribe.

Since creation times, the crows have been designated by their Dreamtime ancestors to be the keepers and controllers of the west wind. This wild wind is the most dreaded of all winds. It can very quickly grow from gentle breeze to roaring gale. It brings with it lightning, thunder and vast rain clouds that can flood the land and cause great hardship for the Aboriginal people.

From earliest memory, the crows have kept this wind confined within a great hollow log. Sometimes some of it escapes through cracks and holes. Then they have to chase it and bring it back to imprison it once more.

But the great log is slowly decaying, as all logs do, and one of the Aborigines' fears is that, one day, the log will not be strong enough to hold the west wind; it will come apart to release a great hurricane that will destroy the whole earth and all things that live upon it.

Among the tribes whose mythology includes this belief, great care is taken not to kill, or in anyway disturb, the black crows. For should this be allowed to happen, disaster is sure to follow.

Echoes of modern ecological warnings reverberate.

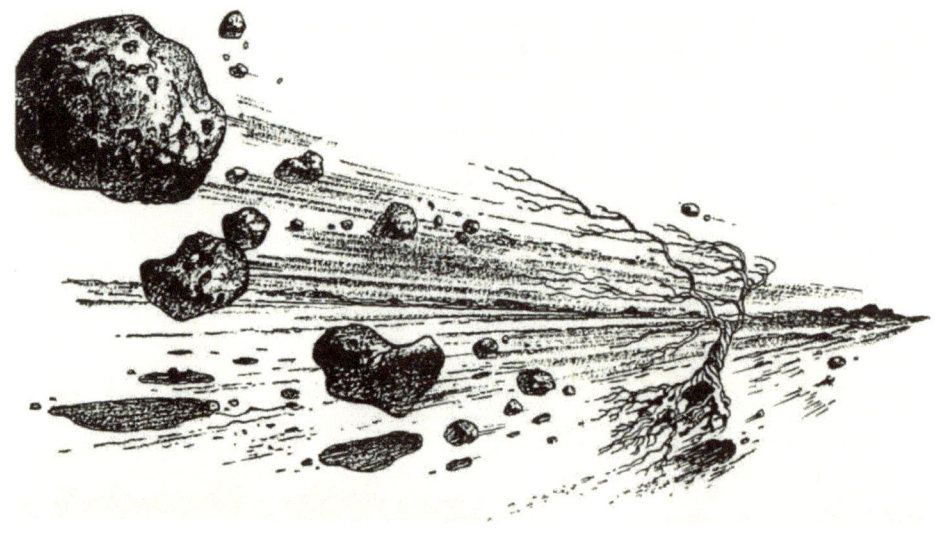

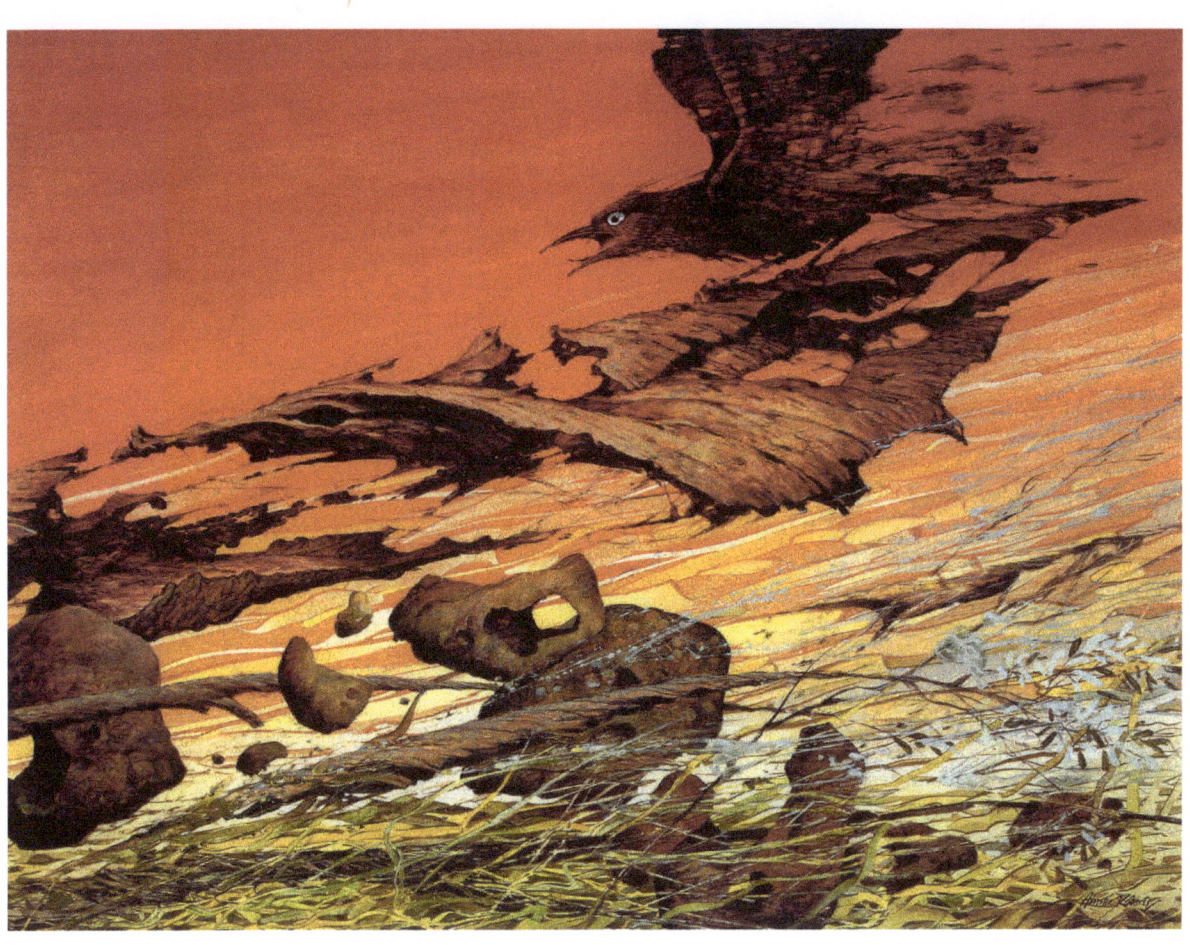

Mr and Mrs Fred Agar

ACKNOWLEDGEMENTS

A number of the myths in this book are printed for the first time. Others have appeared in numerous versions over the past 140 years and every effort has been made to discover their origins. The fact that different tribes used variations of some basic myths and that early European writers interpreted these in many different styles and ways, makes it difficult to ascertain the dates and authors of the first versions to be published in English. We thank those who have granted permission to use the sources as reference. In some cases it has not been possible to trace either the author or the publisher of the original material. The debt to the Australian Aborigines, who originated and perpetuated these myths of their Dreamtime, is most gratefully acknowledged.

SOURCES

McKEOWN, K.C. - *Land of the Byamee*, Randle House, Sydney, 1938.

MATHEWS, R.H. - *Mythology of the Gundungurra*, Folk-Lore Society, London, 1909.

MOUNTFORD, CHARLES P. - *Arnhem Land; Art, Myth and Symbolism*, Melbourne University Press, Melbourne, 1956.

MOUNTFORD, CHARLES P. - *Ayers Rock; Its People, Their Beliefs, Their Art*, Angus & Robertson, Sydney. 1965.

MOUNTFORD, CHARLES P. - Various unpublished manuscripts.

PARKER, K. LANGLOH - *Australian Legendary Tales*, David Nutt, London, 1897.

PECK, C.W. - *Australian Legends*, Stafford & Co., Sydney, 1925.

POOLE, G.G. - *Leigh Creek*, Adelaide, 1946.

REED, A.W. - *Aboriginal Fables*, A.H. & A.W. Reed, Sydney, 1965.

ROBINSON, ROLAND - *Aboriginal Myths and Legends*, Sun Books, Sydney, 1966.

SMITH, W. RAMSAY - *Myths and legends of the Australian Aboriginals*. George G. Harrap, London, 1930.

SPENCER, B. & GILLEN, F.J. - *The Northern Tribes of Central Australia*, Macmillan & Co. Ltd, London, 1904.

TAPLIN, REV. GEORGE TURNER, R. - *South Australian Aboriginal Folklore*, Adelaide, 1879.

WELLS, A.E. - *Australian Jungle Stories*, Northwood Press, Camperdown, Victoria, 1936.

WOODS, J.D. (ed.) - *Stars in the Sky*, Rigby, Adelaide, 1973.

The Native Tribes of South Australia, E.S. Wigg & Son, Adelaide, 1879.